ALL THINGS
GOLF

ALL THINGS GOLF

LESSONS, THOUGHTS, TIPS, REMINDERS AND MEMORIES FROM STAN THIRSK

BY HOWARD RICHMAN

INTRODUCTION BY TOM WATSON

All Things Golf
Lessons, Thoughts, Tips, Reminders and Memories From Stan Thirsk
By Howard Richman

Editor: David Smale
Book design: Kelly Ludwig
Photographs: Rebecca Friend-Jimenez

Published by KANSAS CITY STAR BOOKS
1729 Grand Blvd.
Kansas City, Missouri, USA 64108

First edition
ISBN: 0-9746012-7-6

Printed in the United States of America
by Walsworth Publishing Co., Marceline, Missouri

Requests for permission to make copies of any part of the work should be
mailed to StarInfo, c/o The Kansas City Star, 1729 Grand Blvd., Kansas City,
MO 64108. To order additional copies, call StarInfo (816) 234-4636 and say
"Operator." Or visit our Web site at www.TheKansasCityStore.com.

 KANSAS CITY STAR BOOKS

TABLE OF CONTENTS

INTRODUCTION

Very few human beings you meet in life can be described as "liked by everyone." Stan Thirsk is one of these beautiful people. He is a warm, generous man who smiles as easily as he swings the golf club, and I have never seen him cross with anyone in my life. I have never met a more forgiving man.

Forgiveness and patience are just two of Stan's many qualities that have so positively affected me in the countless hours I have spent in his company as a snot-nosed kid, friend, and fellow competitor. Stan's qualities taught me the important lesson to remain strong, even when my game was sour — a most essential lesson, not only in golf, but in the fuller arena of life itself. "The worm will turn," Stan continually said to me when my game was struggling. It was something I had a difficult time believing. I wanted success too fast, as all kids do, but the patient and forgiving Stan taught me otherwise.

I remember Stan first when I was 11 years old. He was hired as the head professional at the Kansas City Country Club and quickly became a regular in my dad's Saturday afternoon one o'clock game. I took group lessons from Stan in the junior program on Thursday mornings and he occasionally showed us how he could hit it. How those long and powerful shots left a lasting impression on me!

Early the next summer, one Saturday morning, my dad asked me to play in his one o'clock group along with Stan. I couldn't wait. As a 12-year-old, I was more than awed by his reputation that he could drive the 5th green, and I wanted to see it for myself. That day he didn't drive the green, but that one round of golf did a lot to establish a relationship that lasts to this day. It was during that summer my ambition to become a professional golfer was solidified, much to my mother's chagrin.

One of my enduring memories of those wonderful summer Saturdays was the humorous negotiation between Dad and Stan as they needled each other over what Stan was going to score for that round. "Stanley, you get 65, 66, 67, 68, and 69 today for five bucks" (par was 70) my dad would say, meaning that Stan had to shoot 67 to break even; 66 or lower, he'd win, 68 or higher, he'd lose. Stan would either accept or negotiate for higher scores. They would barter back and forth even as the first ball was in the air. Many laughs were had on that first tee, and it taught me the first lesson in betting: all bets are won or lost on the first tee.

The other lasting memory was the time spent by Stan to teach me the game as we played. He truly wanted me to be a great player and I responded to his suggestions with relish. In the end, Stan – always a good negotiator – made out pretty well on his bets with Dad and I benefited in learning from him so many of the fine points of the game. Both of us got richer in so many ways.

The next summer, the course of my life changed forever. An early Monday morning phone call came from Stan. "Tom, this is Stan. Would you like to play with us today?" "Us" was a group of local golf professionals who routinely convened on Mondays (all the clubs were closed this one day of the week) to play golf at one of the pro's clubs. Stan and the revered Duke Gibson, affectionately called "the old man," from Blue Hills Country Club, were to play that day along with a host of other pros that I would also call in later years friends and teachers. Stan backed me as his partner, and with his encouragement, I made a few putts that made him some cash and gave him (and me) bragging rights for that Monday. But, to me, that one day on the golf course with my golfing idols (minus only my dad) solidified my ambition to become a professional golfer. Stan, for that phone call, I will always be indebted to you.

Stan has been like a father to me in many ways. He's a friend, a father, and as I said before, a fellow competitor. He knows and respects the game. He lives the game. He loves the game. I have no greater respect for anyone who has played our wonderful game than I do for Stan.

Hey, Stan, how about 65, 66, 67, 68, and 69?!

— Tom Watson

ACKNOWLEDGMENTS

The first thank you goes to Stan and Audrey Thirsk.

Stan is very much a Kansas City legend. He's too humble to admit it, but it is the truth. His sincerity, friendliness and big heart are traits that make him the man he is. There may be no greater model for man than Stan Thirsk.

I also want to thank Tom Watson for his participation in this book, and for every other time I have called him throughout the years, day or night. He always responded.

Thanks, too, to David Smale, a former colleague at *The Kansas City Star*, who helped guide this project. I also would like to thank Kansas City Country Club and Mission Hills Country Club for their assistance.

Howard Richman

Howard Richman is a sports reporter for The Kansas City Star. *He attended Shawnee Mission West High School in Overland Park, Kan., and Kansas State University in Manhattan, Kan. He started his professional journalism career in 1983 at* The Olathe Daily News *in Olathe, Kan., and joined* The Star *in 1984.*

He covered golf eight years for The Star, *and attended 23 major golf championships in that time, including Tiger Woods' first major championship in the 1997 Masters. He has been a contributor to* Golf World *magazine.*

"I learned by imitation"

THE EARLY YEARS

One of golf's greatest ambassadors entered the world March 22, 1928.

Stan Thirsk was the oldest of five children born to Homer and Clara Ruth Thirsk. He was born in Winfield, a town in southeast Kansas, just miles from the Oklahoma border. A business opportunity took the family to Fruita, Colo., when Stan was 2. This was during the Depression, so it's no shock that the Thirsks lived in simple conditions, in a portable tent, while Homer served as a foreman on the Colorado National Monument road project in far western Colorado. The sound of dynamite, from the road project, was a constant companion.

It could have been worse.

"We always had plenty to eat, and our clothes were clean," Thirsk said. "We may not have had a lot, but when you don't have things, you don't miss them. But I knew we were loved."

Thirsk never went hungry. Meat. Potatoes. Vegetables. Good stuff on the dinner table.

Stan in the late 1930s, with his sisters (from left to right):
Melva Jean, Irma Lee and Dolores Arlene.

"My mom was a great cook. Fried potatoes, mashed potatoes, navy beans, oatmeal in the morning…she could cook," he said.

Money wasn't plentiful, though. "My clothes might have had some patches on them, but they were clean," Thirsk said.

His dad drove an old Ford. "It got us where we were going," he said.

Thirsk recalled how badly he wanted a bicycle. He mostly kept the idea to himself.

"I didn't say much about it. My mom sold eggs to the grocery store, she saved, and she got me that bicycle," Thirsk said. "I was probably 8 or 9. A blue Western Flyer."

One day Stan was riding his most prized possession to school. He wasn't a great driver.

"I slipped off of it, and it hurt me," he said. "I don't want to go into where it hurt me."

En route to school, Thirsk became accustomed to strange, scary noises.

"We had to walk through sagebrush and cactus, and there were rattlesnakes," he said. "I made plenty of noise, so they knew I was there."

When Stan turned 12, the Thirsks were on the move again, landing in Wichita, Kan. Stan spent his summers in Winfield, which was about an hour away. Winfield is where the game of golf infiltrated his blood.

He stayed in Winfield with his aunt and uncle, Mickey

and Les Hedges, who belonged to the local country club. They would bring Stan to the club three or four times a week.

"When I watched them play, I got excited," he said. "He (his uncle) was terrible, but I knew if you could do it right, you could have fun with it."

Thirsk said he was "thin as a 1-iron" when he first became a club professional. It didn't keep him from developing a fluid swing.

Neither wind, rain or even snow could keep Thirsk from his appointed round—
of golf. Nineteen-year-old Thirsk spent his early years playing at Sim Park.

Besides, being a caddie beat the alternative.

Stan spent too many summer days doing chores at home. He fed the horses and the cows every morning and every evening. He learned to hoe the cornfields. That was quite an experience.

"I broke the handle two times," he said, "and my father said if I did it again, he'd break the rest of it over my rear end."

Planting potatoes became part of Stan's repertoire. So did peeling them, in the cellar, sometimes more than six hours a day.

"That's a lot of potatoes," he said.

One summer when he returned from his aunt's and uncle's house, Stan told his parents he wanted to become a caddie. His days of peeling potatoes were coming to an end.

Their house was located on North St. Paul Street in Wichita, separated from Sim Park Golf Course by the Arkansas River. Unless he wanted to challenge the water and swim across, Stan had to take the long way around to get there. He didn't like that alternative either because he couldn't wait to get to the course.

"If the river was low, you could try to walk across it," he said, "but I wouldn't try to swim it because I couldn't swim a lick. When my dad went to work, usually he went the other way from the golf course, so I'd walk it. It took about half an hour. I couldn't wait to get there."

Caddies could play Sim Park for free Mondays from sunup to noon. On summer days, Stan would arrive at the course by no later than 5:30 a.m.

"We could play 36 holes easy," he said.

On other days, it cost caddies 75 cents. Those days, Stan caddied. It was how he learned to love the game. Two men in particular had as much to do with his introduction to golf as anybody.

"A couple of guys who ran a night club until 4 in the morning would be there to play golf at 6," Thirsk recalled, "and they were there so early, the pro let them play out of one bag. They'd play 18 holes in 2½ hours. Caddie fees at the club were 75 cents, but these guys gave me $4 and bought me lunch and a snack in between, too. So I really was living high on the hog."

Thirsk says he never lacked for confidence when he toted the bag.

"If I do say so myself, I was a great caddie. Because I loved it," he said. "I was always out in front of them (golfers he was caddying for), and they liked that. I tried to be polite, and I kept my mouth shut. I was there to do a job. They would praise me. I just wanted to do a good job and please them."

Mostly, he wanted to learn. Thirsk watched the players like a hawk, paying attention to every little detail. He was hungry to learn the game, and this was his classroom.

"I watched how they put their hands on the club, how smooth they swung, how they stood up to the ball," he said. "I learned a lot about people and how you control your emotions. One of them would get hotheaded, and he usually ended up losing. I picked up on that."

So when he would go and play, Thirsk attempted to employ all of the things he had witnessed, and make them work for him.

"I loved going out there when I could play and see if I could control the ball and make it go where I wanted it to go," he said.

Observing golf greats Byron Nelson, Sam Snead and Ben Hogan certainly helped. The three legends participated in exhibitions at Sim Park and other courses in Wichita. The youngster soaked in every shot.

"Hogan sure knew how to work the ball," Thirsk said. "They don't do that now. Everything is a slugfest."

Nelson and Jug McSpaden, best known in their heyday as "the Gold Dust Twins," were Stan's favorites. After watching one of their exhibitions at Sim Park, Stan, then a teenager, shot a 1-over-par 36. It was a breakthrough for him, and the beginning of bigger and better things.

"I learned by imitation," Thirsk said. "I could see how their swings accelerated gradually, without a sudden change in the direction of the backswing and the downswing. When you watch the best, you can learn."

The only learning Thirsk wanted to accomplish was on a golf course. That's the reason he quit high school early and never received a diploma.

He doesn't regret it.

"I probably got a better education from people in the real world," he said.

Instead of school, Stan was hired as an assistant pro at Sim Park. Still 16 at the time, he had hoped to enter a city tournament in Wichita. At about the same time, he was helping build a driving range on the east side of town, and someone informed the United States Golf Association about it. The USGA told Thirsk if he was making money in golf, he would have to be classified as a professional, which prevented him from playing in the tournament.

"I was no more a pro than a jet pilot," Thirsk said, "but I had to turn pro when I was 16. I opened and closed seven days a week. I started making $60 a week. I eventually got up to $100."

Working at the course also helped him improve his game. Thirsk took a club member who was a barber by day and won a pro-guest event right after he started.

"People told me I was really good, but I didn't think about it," Thirsk said.

Thirsk eventually decided the money simply wasn't good enough in golf, especially when he married Audrey and started having a family. He went to work for Boeing from 1948-56 as an expediter. During that time, he became reacquainted with MacGregor golf sales representative

Johnny Walker. In late 1955, Walker relayed to Thirsk that there was an assistant's opening at Mission Hills Country Club in the Kansas City area. The money would be good

FOURBALL FINALISTS—W. R. Galbraith, left, and Stan Thirsk, second from left, are shown being congratulated after winning The Wichita Beacon-PGA fourball tournament Sunday at Meadow Lark b ythe runners-up—Jay Kile second from right, and Chandler Wade, right.

Thirsk's first tournament win earned him a photo in the *Wichita Beacon*.

enough to handle the job and his family.

"I took that job, and from there, it just kept getting better for me," Thirsk said.

That's when Thirsk truly began to teach the game. Too often at Sim Park he was stuck behind the counter. There were days like that as well at Mission Hills, but not as many. All he really wanted was to teach and play.

"I'm lucky nobody filed a malpractice suit against me," Thirsk said with a laugh. "I learned from watching the best players, like Snead, Nelson and Hogan, and I was trying to pass that on. I knew when you changed the man's hands on the club, that changed everything."

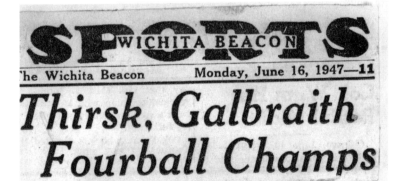

SPORTS
WICHITA BEACON

'he Wichita Beacon   Monday, June 16, 1947—11

Thirsk, Galbraith Fourball Champs

Westlinkers Lose to Sim Park Duo

Young Stan Thirsk and the vet-
ran W. R. Galbraith were the 1947
Wichita Beacon-PGA fourball

Thirsk began making headlines at a young age.

T I P S

T H E   B A S I C S

Want to improve? Here's Thirsk's checklist of how to help get you there.

- ✓ **Concentrate on the grip**
- ✓ **Posture**
- ✓ **Balance**
- ✓ **Proper set-up**

"You'd be amazed at how much better you could get if you pay attention to those things all the time," Thirsk says.

(The tips in this book assume a righthanded player. For lefthanders, the tips are the same, just from the opposite side.)

T H E   G R I P

No. 1 in my book is the grip. You have to start with the proper grip. No doubt, it's the biggest flaw in most golfers I have taught.

It feels right, and it's what they've gotten used to. There's nothing exciting about putting your hands on the club, but if you don't do it right, you're making things worse right from the start.

The only time you should change your grip is when you putt.

There are two parts to the grip: position of the hands on the club, and feel. Never grip it tight. That makes for an enormous amount of tension. It takes away direction and distance. There's no way you can feel the club head weight by squeezing it. A death grip never gives you the sense of feel you need.

Just remember, there's not supposed to be any tension that might lock up the joints. On a scale of 1 to 10, with 1 being lightest, you ought to be around a 2 or 3 in terms of grip pressure. That goes for putting as well.

I see a lot of golfers at a 10, partly because they're holding the club wrong. They don't have it positioned properly, so they have to hang on tight to hold it.

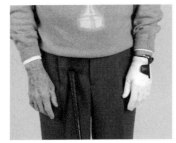
Let your hands hang naturally.

The club lies at the base of the fingers, not in the palm.

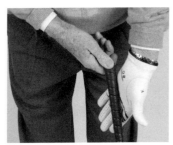
Wrap your lead hand around the club first.

When you start holding the club correctly, you'll start getting a feel for the club head. It's got to be down in the fingers, with most of the pressure being in your baby finger, middle finger and ring finger of your left hand.

The "V" between your index finger and thumb should point to your opposite shoulder.

David Duval had trouble with his grip. Tom (Watson) and I were watching him at the (2002) PGA at Hazeltine. His tee ball started dead left, hit on the left side in the trees, in a practice round. His left hand grip was too strong.

Bring the other hand under the first hand.

If you grip it too lightly, where you let the club go or let it slip around in the fingers, you have no control over the swing, meaning you lose distance and direction.

You don't have much margin for error with grip and

The "V" again points up to the same shoulder.

grip pressure. Work until you get it right. Stay aware of it all the time, and don't ever take it for granted.

If you don't play for a couple of weeks, re-establish feel again. It starts with the grip.

You can either interlock your fingers or overlap the pinkie over the index finger (pictured).

POSTURE / BALANCE

Assume the right posture so you're on balance when you start. You've got to have your balance right when you start so you can maintain it while you are in motion.

Bend at the sockets and unlock your knees. Your spine goes forward and it drops your arms in front of you. As you flex your knees, it allows you to set the club behind the ball.

Don't sit down. When you sit down, you have to slump over. You can't make that swing.

Bend at the hip socket.

If you're on balance, you'll have your power. If you're not on balance, your swing is dead.

Don't stand over the ball like a statue, with your legs concrete. Your balance should never be on the back of your heels.

Your feet should be about even with the outside of your shoulders. Don't be too wide or too narrow in your stance. If you get too wide, you can't have proper weight shift. If you're too narrow, you're too top heavy and off balance.

Good balance comes from correct posture. It starts with a slight bend from your hip sockets, enough that your arms fall in front of you, and it tilts your shoulders forward. That makes you stick your

Your spine goes forward and drops your arms in front of you.

Flex your knees slightly. Your feet should be even with the outside of your shoulders.

buttocks out over your heels, and it unlocks your knees so you're not standing stiff-legged.

When you flex your knees, your balance will go from your heels to the balls of your feet. If you watch the good players, their balance and posture is always perfect. You don't see them losing their balance when they swing.

Ladies have a hard time accepting sticking their bottoms out over their heels. They've been taught that it's not lady-like. I once taught a lady who was not very thrilled with the idea. I told her it wouldn't look as bad as she imagined. She told me she would try five swings the way I was teaching her. If she didn't see improvement, she wouldn't pursue it any more.

The very first ball she hit went right down the middle of the fairway. It was one of the best shots she hit. Very subtly, she looked over at me and said, "I can live with this."

"Good players go the same speed, every single time."

KNOW YOUR LIMITS, AND OTHER LIFE-LESSONS

Golf legend Tom Watson learned the game at Kansas City Country Club from his father, Raymond, Bob Willits and Stan Thirsk.

Thirsk learned from Tex Consolver, the club pro at Sim Park in Wichita, Kansas. But his dad, Homer, may have taught Thirsk the most memorable lesson.

Thirsk was playing with his father, when the youngster tried to prove that he could clear a huge tree down the left side of the fairway. The young Thirsk took a 9-iron and attempted to complete the feat with a swift swing.

Bad decision. The ball rattled around in the leaves, and plopped to the base of the trunk. Then came bad decision No. 2. In his anger, Thirsk wheeled and heaved the club. The club struck a man on the leg on the adjacent 15th green.

"I knew it had to sting," Thirsk said.

The victim's response?

Even Tom Watson (with Thirsk), one of the all-time greats, had to learn what he was capable of doing, and then adjust his game accordingly.

"He started after me," Thirsk said. "When he got there, my dad said, 'Hold it. I'll take care of this.'"

The punishment was a 45-minute session in the family garage.

"We had a little 'conference.' He was bouncing me off the wall," Thirsk said. "He didn't abuse me. But he did tell me losing your temper is no good. He shoved me against the car. He said, 'You don't like that very much, do you?' He told me how much the man I hit with the club didn't like that, either."

Thirsk never will forget the lesson his father taught him that day in the garage. It also served as an important training tool he would use for years in his own golfing career and when he taught his pupils.

"I was trying to do something I wasn't capable of doing when I hit that 9-iron," he said. "It turned out to be one of those lessons that sticks with you."

On one of his ventures onto the PGA Tour, Thirsk experienced another lesson in not trying to do too much, and this time it almost cost him his life.

Thirsk made a run in the Bob Hope Classic in 1965. When the tournament concluded, Thirsk remembers driving his caddie to the bus depot before taking off for KC in his car sometime around 4:30 p.m.

"My caddie told me he had heard Julius Boros tell somebody I was a comer. It made me feel pretty good," Thirsk said. "I was trying to prove to myself that I could compete."

With that information dancing in his head, a fired up Thirsk began the trek home. He recalls stopping in Phoenix for a cup of coffee and sandwich, and soon it was dark. The adrenaline that had flowed through him now was nearly drained, and Thirsk almost paid the consequences.

"I was driving through Globe (Arizona, located east of Phoenix), and I dozed off. I woke up when I heard the gravel

Thirsk has spent his entire career helping golfers of all levels make the most of the talent that they have.

kicking up," Thirsk said. "It was flying up on my car. I got back under control. The first chance I got, I stopped for more coffee."

And a motel.

The next day, Thirsk encountered an ice storm in Oklahoma City. He saw pickups, motor trailers and cars in ditches as he crept along the interstate at 10 miles per hour. That was simple stuff compared to the dozing-off incident.

"I thanked the Lord for waking me up because there's no good place to drive off the road," Thirsk said.

Thirsk can't imagine a better drive through life. Along the way he developed the way he wanted to live it.

"This is all I wanted to do since I was young. I was really very fortunate to be able to do what I loved so much," Thirsk said. "To be able to do what you want is important, but the thing is, when it comes time to tell all this goodbye and leave this world and go to the next one, that's what I'm more interested in.

"Byron Nelson said he wanted to go to Heaven. I do, too. You've got to live your life in a way God wants you to live your life. That's what I'm trying to do, so I can make the cut upstairs."

Thirsk made many cuts as a player. He taught himself, then watched others to validate what he had done.

Thirsk spent hours putting and chipping. "I would watch other people, and I realized what I was doing was orthodox," he said. "I knew I had to play my ball back in my stance, hands ahead, weight over on my left. I made it a routine."

The hardest aspect of the game for Thirsk to learn? Rhythm.

"I had to learn to swing the club at the same speed all the way through. When the heat is on, you've got to do that well," he said. "When I began playing, and I would be on my downswing, the sparks flew. But I got after it, worked on it, and learned you would get a ticket for speeding."

When Thirsk was tied for the PGA Championship lead after one round in 1972 with a 68, his rhythm played a role in the second-day debacle. Thirsk shot an 82, barely made the cut, and he knew exactly what went wrong.

"I didn't change anything," he said, "but I didn't have the same rhythm, and I hit some shots that were really bad. I had an eight on a par-4 and a six on another par-4. That's lack of rhythm. Good players go the same speed, every single time."

Patience is a crucial part in golf, and learning it is a key for success, Thirsk believes.

"I learned to be patient by disappointment. Sometimes you want something really bad, and try to force things. You've got to be patient and earn it," he said.

"You've got to persevere. Because if you don't succeed the first time, you've still got to keep at it, keep your goals high."

Thirsk always strived to improve his pupils.

"Not only did I want to be a better player, but I also wanted to give the people I taught the right information to become better players," Thirsk said. "You can get a lot of information. But you've got to know what is true. I owe it to the game, to the people who come to me, to make them better faster."

T I P S

ALIGNMENT

When you play golf, you stand to the side of the ball to hit it. Your body lines—knees, hips, shoulders—need to be parallel to your target line. You'll see players go into their routine, which you also have to have, standing behind the ball and picturing their swing, flying the ball to the target.

Body line parallel to the target line is the key here.

Go to a PGA Tour event, and at the practice tee, they'll have clubs on the ground to make sure they are lining up properly. They lay a couple of clubs parallel for the target line and for where they want their body to be.

When practicing, place two clubs parallel to the direction you want the ball to go.

Always put a couple of clubs down when you practice.

When you are on the practice tee, it helps you practice in the right manner. It ingrains good habits, something that stays with you out on the course. I've seen people make a good swing, but they aimed their body—instead of the clubface—at the target.

Ball position is forward when you are hitting your driver. As the club gets a little bit shorter, ball position goes more toward the middle of your stance, and the swing path gets steeper. As the club gets longer, you stand further from the ball. Weight goes more toward the right foot and leg, the ball is more forward-center.

Most of the time, we see people come over the ball too much. For example, a player takes the club back too far inside and swings from the inside out over the ball and comes back in, so his path is going left.

Visualize where you want the ball to go.

This will keep you in proper alignment to produce an even swing.

THE FEEL OF THE GAME

One rule I ask all my students, and myself, is to play the game by feel.

What I teach one person may not be what I teach the next person. Each person is a little bit different, but one thing everyone has to have is a routine.

Your body chemistry changes one day to the next. When your fingers feel hot and puffy, you're not going to get much of a feel. Other days, you'll feel great, and you hit the ball perfectly. Feel is so important because it changes. Just keep trying to do things over and over until you get the feel and consistency that is working for you that day.

HOLD YOUR HEAD HIGH

When I hear somebody tell a golfer to keep his head down when standing over the ball, I shake my head.

Keeping your head down is a no-no.

So, what then? Your chin always has to be up because it restricts your swing if your chin is buried in your chest. If you are hunched over too much, it prevents you from making the turn, and hinders your backswing.

In keeping your head up (there should be a straight line from your tailbone to the back of your neck), you'll have room for your shoulders at the apex of your backswing.

THE KANSAS CITY COUNTRY CLUB

MEMBERS AND GUESTS ONLY

"You put your members ahead of everything."

THE COUNTRY CLUB
LIFE—THE TRUTH

It's the middle 1950s. A salesman for MacGregor, a golf manufacturing company, happened to be at Sim Park Golf Course. That visit by the salesman changed Stan Thirsk's life forever.

"They needed an assistant (club pro) at Mission Hills Country Club," Thirsk said.

Mission Hills had a need and wanted Thirsk. The club got its man. Thirsk started March 1, 1956, at Mission Hills. It was a Sunday. Head club professional Billy Mathews greeted Thirsk on his first day, but didn't stick around very long.

"He gave me the key, turned around, and said, 'See ya Tuesday,'" Thirsk recalled.

The first character that comes to Thirsk's mind at Mission Hills was The Chief.

"He weighed 300 pounds. Wide and strong," Thirsk said. "He was a caddie. He would carry four bags down the fairway.

The entrance to Kansas City Country Club leads to one of the oldest and most prestigious clubs in the Kansas City area.

The current 11th hole at Mission Hills Country Club is a par 3 that runs parallel to Shawnee Mission Parkway. Thirsk says you have to have good judgment on distance to do well because of the bunkers.

He didn't say much, and I certainly didn't argue with him about anything."

The golf course at Mission Hills isn't much different than Kansas City Country Club, Thirsk says.

"It's like KCCC, only a little shorter," he said. "You had to play good shots. You had to hit hooks, fades, had to hit it high, had to hit it low. It didn't play long, but I remember using all the clubs in my bag to play it."

The membership at Mission Hills included some CEOs from area companies. Pro golfer Gene Littler befriended one of the members, and Thirsk remembers him playing the course on occasion.

Thirsk's best score at Mission Hills: 63. His favorite hole: No. 11, which is now No. 16.

"It was well over 400 yards," he said. In the summer, against the south wind and a dogleg left, it was tough. You'd hit your tee shot down there and you couldn't see all the green because it was down in a swale."

Thirsk said Mathews was wonderful to work for. He recalled how Mathews used a tennis ball attached to a string to teach. He would have his pupil swing the string with the tennis ball back and forth, and it had to remain taut to emulate the swing he wanted from them. If it crinkled or buckled, it meant the swing wasn't on a smooth, straight path.

"I learned a lot from watching Bill," Thirsk said. "He placed his hands on the club properly, and that was the first thing you had to do. There was nothing I

Souvenir

"Duke" Gibson

Stan Thirsk

Children's Mercy Hospital

Century Club

Exhibition

GOLF MATCH

and Clinic

1 p.m. August 10, 1964

BLUE HILLS COUNTRY CLUB

1500 W. Burning Tree Dr. - 127 & State Line

Kansas City, Missouri

BETSY RAWLS, LPGA

JUDY KIMBALL, LPGA

vs

DUKE GIBSON, PGA

STAN THIRSK, PGA

Judy Kimball

Betsy Rawls

The second annual Century Club Golf Match is a success in advance due to the fine response of all the SPONSORS, PATRONS and those who have so liberally contributed to our fund. Mrs. Roy D. North, president.

One of Thirsk's favorite events was playing in the charity tournament with fellow club pro Duke Gibson, and LPGA players Betsy Rawls and Judy Kimball.

Mission Hills Country Club is where it all began in Kansas City for Stan Thirsk.

didn't like about Bill. He was kind and patient and I never heard him say anything bad about anyone."

Not only did the members and co-workers have an impact on Thirsk, he had an impact on those around him. Thirsk called one Davy Crockett. Actually, his real name was David Hendricks. Hendricks, who worked in the caddie barn at Mission Hills when Thirsk came to work there, recalls how Thirsk burst onto the scene.

"Stan was real energetic, and always a lot of fun," Hendricks said. "He was always pleasant, and had a grin on his face every time you talked with him."

Hendricks caddied for Thirsk once in an event at Indian Hills Country Club, and three times Thirsk hit shots in ground under repair. Each time, Hendricks used what Thirsk called his "foot mashie" to kick the ball to safer ground.

"The third time, he caught on," Hendricks said, "and he told me, 'Crockett, quit teeing my ball up; people are going to get suspicious.'"

After nearly five years at Mission Hills, Thirsk took the next step in his career. If the move to Mission Hills was considered big, this one was a real whopper.

On January 1, 1961, Thirsk began what would be a fruitful and lengthy stay at arguably the city's most prestigious club, Kansas City Country Club. Bob Willits, Larry Smith and Sam Giles were instrumental in convincing Thirsk that KCCC was right for him. But the home course for people like the

Kempers, Henry Bloch and, of course, legendary golf champion Tom Watson, nearly missed out on Thirsk.

Wakonda Country Club in Des Moines, Iowa, also was attempting to lure Thirsk. The same day Thirsk accepted the job from Kansas City Country Club, Wakonda called and made an offer. Too late, however.

"Wakonda would have been great," Thirsk said, "but I would have had to move."

Thirsk never moved again. He stayed at Kansas City Country Club until 1993, enjoying some of his finest years. People like Rev. Billy Graham, Lee Trevino and Gay Brewer played there. Brewer won the 1967 Masters, but he lost some dough at KCCC.

"He got into a game with some members who had pretty good handicaps," Thirsk said.

Some moments stand out like they happened yesterday.

"We were going down No. 10, and one of the guys in our group went down to the right side where he'd sliced it," Thirsk said. "He decided to relieve himself up against a tree. The guy who was hitting last shanked one. It caromed off the tree into this man's crotch. He tinkled all over himself."

Three cart mishaps in more than 30 years on the job isn't a bad ratio. Thirsk can recall every one of them.

"Two men said the cart got away from them, on the right side of No. 11, short of the 150-yard marker," he said. "It gets real steep as you go down to the 14th tee, and the cart hit a tree at the bottom."

The total damage: $700. The golfers paid for it.

An older member drove a cart into a bunker one day at sunset near No. 6. Thirsk waited until daylight to retrieve it.

On the eighth hole, a ladies group watched in horror as their cart got away from them. The cart glided into a creek. Nobody was hurt.

Thirsk remembers a time or two of broken windows from people playing No. 9. If a shot caromed off the cart path, it possibly could find the path leading to the grille room.

"We finally got double-plated glass that wouldn't break as easily," he said.

The club pool also is adjacent to No. 9, and it sometimes got in the way.

"You could get off base and hit it in there from either No. 9 or No. 6," Thirsk said. "Thank goodness no one got hurt, at least that I can remember."

Irritated might be the best way to describe a homeowner who lived to the left of No. 14 years ago. If you hit it left on the par-3, the man's home was a target. His house became a receptacle for golf balls, and a broken window or two.

"He got a little upset," Thirsk said, "but we tried to tell him in a nice way the golf course was there before his house."

As for some of his members' faces, they remain dominant in Thirsk's mind. Like the little girl he called Oops.

"When she missed a shot badly, she'd say, 'Oops!'"

Country Club Picks Stan Thirsk To Fill Golf Professional Spot

By Dick Mackey.
(A Member of The Star's Sports Staff.)

KANSAS CITY Country club's quest for a new golf professional ended yesterday with the announcement that Stan Thirsk, assistant pro at Mission Hills, has been named to succeed Paul Wieler.

The appointment, effective January 1, was announced by S. E. Giles, greens chairman. Weiler, who has gone into private business, had announced his resignation earlier this year.

For Thirsk, at 32, it marks another high point in a golfing career that, oddly enough, began when he literally was forced to turn pro at 16.

At that time, Stan was a part-time tractor driver at a driving range in Wichita. When Thirsk attempted to enter a local amateur tournament, he was informed he could not be classified as an amateur because his income was derived from golf.

U. S. G. A. Stops Him.

Thirsk objected and wrote to the United States Golf association, explaining his position. When the U. S. G. A. backed up the original ruling, Stan, at 16, found himself a pro—whether he liked it or not.

Thirsk had figured on a career in golf, but at 16 he felt the move was a little premature. Nevertheless, since then —with the exception of a stint with an aircraft company—he has been in golf. Prior to coming to Mission Hills in April, 1956, Stan was an assistant to Tex Consolver in Wichita.

Stan, whose physical dimensions (5-11, 160) resemble a

Stan Thirsk.

one-iron, is admittedly thrilled over the appointment.

"The only tough thing about it," he commented yesterday, "is that I hate to leave Billy (Mathews, Mission Hills' pro). As far as I'm concerned, he's tops."

As yet, Mathews has not decided who he will hire to replace Stan.

He May Play Tour.

At K. C. C. C., Thirsk, who has gained the reputation as a long-ball hitter, will be free to join the winter tour for part of the off season. That, however, will come later. At the present time, he's busy winding up affairs at Mission Hills and opening up shop at the Country club.

Working with him will be Casey Morgan, John Foster and Joe Sullivan.

Stan is married and has two daughters, Gayrene, 11, and Jodell, 2.

This article appeared in *The Kansas City Star* when Thirsk was named the head professional at Kansas City Country Club.

A young man named Biff never could get the grip down and Thirsk's attempts to teach him were met with futility.

"He'd swing and try to hit the ball as hard as he could. I told him not to lunge and try to kill it," Thirsk said. "He said, 'Stan, I don't want to listen to all that stuff. I just want to hit it.'"

Thirsk said the young boy eventually grew into a decent player.

"As he got older, he got wiser," Thirsk said with a grin.

No doubt Thirsk has a sense of humor.

Chuck Frisbie and his sons, Ross and Andrew, belonged to Kansas City Country Club, and they were headed outside the area for a getaway to play. Thirsk had a piece of advice (with tongue firmly placed in cheek) for the boys before they departed.

"Stan said, 'Take the bag tag off (Chuck's bag) because we don't want anyone to know where he plays,'" Frisbie said.

Thirsk joked with the boys, "Do me a favor. Don't watch him swing because I don't want you imitating what he does."

In reality, the two men had the utmost respect for each other. Thirsk showed it by his actions.

"I had to get my lesson in early because I had to get to the office," Frisbie said, "so we'd meet at 8 a.m. It wasn't horribly early, but he was going above and beyond to come in earlier than he normally would just for me.

"I've enjoyed his friendship, his tenacity and his ability to stand there and look at this awful golf swing."

It's no surprise that more than a decade after he retired,

the strongest memories are of the members he served. Some were humorous, others were heart-rending. All were memorable.

A member once strolled into the pro shop, requesting one Izod sock. "I started laughing. He started laughing," Thirsk said. "I said, 'I don't have any one-legged members.' So he bought one, and I gave the other one to my greens chairman, who said he'd give the sock to his dog so he could chew it up."

So, why did the man need just one sock?

"I guess he'd lost the other one," Thirsk chuckled.

That same man constantly grilled Thirsk as to why it cost $4.50 for a golf glove. When the man made a trip to England, one of the first people he saw when he returned was Thirsk.

"He walked in the shop, and didn't acknowledge my greeting," Thirsk said. "He said, 'I got this pair of gloves for $2 more than what you charged for one.' I said, 'It must have cost you $10,000 to go to England to get those gloves.' He didn't think that was too funny."

Another member, who had attended a church retreat, returned to Thirsk, refreshed and convinced the time away did him good.

"He said, 'I feel really good. I want you to come watch me hit some chip shots.'

"We went out there, I rolled a ball out, and on the very first one he rolled a divot over it. He just covered the ball with it," Thirsk said. "He didn't touch the ball.

"I think he needed to go meditate and to retreat a little bit more."

One of the club's members who was dying of cancer played in an event with Thirsk. They rode together, and the man asked Thirsk a favor when he drove the cart. Instead of pulling up so the man had to get out on the right side, walk around the back to get his club and hit the ball, he requested Thirsk make it easier for him.

"He said, 'Stan, from here on, I want you to pull up on the left side of the ball. That way, I can just fall out of the cart, pull a club out, hit it and fall back in the cart.'

"Later we walked off No. 7, our team was 11-under, and I got excited for him. In my excitement, we hit our tee balls on No. 8, and I pulled him up on the right side of his ball. He said, 'Stan, I'm only going to tell you one more time...'"

Thirsk's team won that day. The member died not too long afterward.

"When he died, the gift certificate for winning was still in his locker," Thirsk said.

Thirsk's normal days started with lessons from 9 until noon. Lunch in the grille room? That never changed.

"I was there 32 years, and I had a cheeseburger every day," he said, "and the black bean soup if it was available. Of course, you had to top it off with a black and white (a cup of ice cream with chocolate syrup)."

Six of Thirsk's eight holes in one occurred at No. 2 at Kansas City Country Club.

Perhaps it wasn't the Atkins Diet. But it didn't fatten up Thirsk.

"I never gained an ounce," he said. "Stayed as thin as a 1-iron."

The prettiest hole at KCCC, Thirsk said, was No. 16. It's a dogleg left with a row of walnut trees down the right, pin oaks and bunkers along the left.

The most difficult green? The ninth, especially if it was slicked up. You didn't want to be in the bunker on the right side. The green falls from the right side to the left.

"One year we had amateur qualifying, and the pin was on the right front," Thirsk recalled, "and the wind came up and dried it out. If you hit it up there and it didn't go in, it would roll right back down to your feet."

Thirsk posted eight holes-in-one at Kansas City Country

Club (six on No. 2), one on No. 6 and one on 14. His best score was a 61 from the silver tees, with three 62s from the reds.

The saddest part of his tenure at Kansas City Country Club, Thirsk said, was standing by helplessly as Dutch elm trees died in the 1960s and 1970s.

"They were big, beautiful trees. We must have lost at least 800 of them," Thirsk said. "They were huge, in strategic places. They made you play shots."

Thirsk was most focused on his pupils. He wanted to make sure they were ready to play whatever shots they faced. He called them like he saw them. One of them, Mary Jane Barnes, could have taken Thirsk's words the wrong way.

Barnes began taking lessons from him in 1962 at Kansas City Country Club, when the practice area was located where the tennis courts are now. She'll never forget his honesty about her game.

Thirsk's favorite hole at Kansas City Country Club is No. 16.

"He said, 'I don't think you'll ever hit it a long way.' He told me to keep working on my short game," Barnes said. "He really encouraged me. He made me believe, 'Doggone it, I can do it.'"

Instead of being concerned that she wouldn't boom tee shots, Barnes focused on the essentials. As long as she drove it in the fairway, she would be okay if all other facets of her game fell into place.

Obviously, they did.

Barnes went on to win 16 club championships. She won't take all the spotlight for her success.

"I credit my love of the game to Stan Thirsk," she said. "I would not have been as interested, or as good."

Barnes said Thirsk had an uncanny way of pinpointing any problem she had in her game.

"He'd fix my short game in 15 minutes," she said. "He would spot things, whether it was in the setup, takeaway, whatever. He spotted it immediately."

Even to this day, Barnes still sees Thirsk for lessons at Blue Hills Country Club.

"It's a privilege for me," Barnes said.

There were others who made Kansas City Country Club a success. Office manager Dorothea Buschmann was as important as anyone to making the club click, Thirsk said.

"She knew how to take care of things," he said. "I'd get ready to go home, but I'd stop first and have a cup of coffee with her. She knew how to take care of members. She knew to put them first."

The membership was close at Kansas City Country Club, and that made for a cozy environment.

"You knew everybody. We had maybe 300 members, and you knew each other," Thirsk said. "That made it warm."

Perhaps the zaniest moment he encountered at Kansas City Country Club, Thirsk said, involved his greens committee chairman. The man, Thirsk said, was adamant about placing a sign between the No. 1 tee and No. 9 green to inform players there should be no pitching, putting or chipping in that area.

"People would take their wedge or putter and use it at the ninth green before they teed off," Thirsk said. "They'd scuff it up and not repair it. He didn't want all of that wear and tear.

"I helped him put the sign up. He came back later that day and got ready to play. I looked out, and the first thing I saw was him pitching to the ninth green. He flat forgot he had put that sign up. I brought it to his attention. He was embarrassed.

"'We're creatures of habit, aren't we?' he said. He was the nicest man to come down the pike. But he just flat forgot."

Thirsk gave lessons at Kansas City Country Club, more than he can count, but one in particular that he never got to finish remains lodged in his memory bank.

"I had a little girl. Her mom and dad wanted her to take

up golf," Thirsk said. "So we went up to the lesson tee, and I put her hands in the right position 40 different times because she kept taking her hands out of the correct position. The next week, she did the same thing again. She'd just drop her hands off."

Thirsk was befuddled until the girl told him she really had no interest at all in golf.

"She said she wanted to go to the pool. That's where her friends all were," Thirsk said, "so I took her down there. I didn't want to waste her parents' money anymore."

Kansas City Country Club is custom-made for players who want to become excellent, Thirsk said. It's tight and requires accurate drives. You have to keep it straight because of the narrow fairways. The greens are small, with subtle little breaks everywhere.

Thirsk especially loves the par 3s there. In fact, Thirsk believes it's almost like playing at Augusta National Golf Club, site of the Masters.

"If you get in certain places above the holes, you can't control your speed," he said.

The beauty of Kansas City Country Club in the spring awakened Thirsk's senses.

"We had a lot of flowering trees, peach trees and maples that turned gold and red in the fall," he said.

Although some extremely wealthy and influential people belonged to Kansas City Country Club, Thirsk doesn't remember any of them being conceited.

"You might've thought they'd have their noses up in the air, but they weren't trying to impress anyone," Thirsk said. "They didn't have to. They had money, no doubt about it. But they didn't put on any aires. I loved their attitudes. I can't think of anyone who was real bad."

Most of Thirsk's time was spent making sure his members enjoyed every minute of their experience. He believed in that every day he went to work.

"You put your members ahead of everything," he said. "These people wanted to relax. They'd been working hard at the office all week. You wanted to take care of them when they came to see you. You wanted to make them feel like this was their second home."

Anybody who played golf at Kansas City Country Club in the Thirsk years surely remembers the Stan Am.

Each spring and summer, Thirsk would play with three members of the club, and they would keep standings on which team posted the best score. It gave Thirsk the opportunity to become more familiar with members. It'd be a regular occurrence on Saturdays and Sundays. Winners, at the conclusion of the Stan Am, earned gift certificates in the pro shop.

Bob Sawyer recalled the day in the Stan Am when Thirsk shot a 61.

"He was hitting his irons 8, 10, 12 feet away," Sawyer said.

"He made it look so easy. I was lucky enough to be there for it."

Sawyer said all the club members were lucky to be around when Thirsk was part of their lives.

"He touched an awful lot of lives. He had a way of making you feel you were the most important person in the world at that moment in time," Sawyer said.

The club had a huge going-away celebration for Thirsk, and Sawyer still is amazed at Thirsk's devotion to his trade, even when his time there was finished.

"Stan's in a greeting line," Sawyer said, "and I stopped to wish him the very best. One of the things he always told me was, 'Bob, you're gripping the club too tightly.' Well, I shake his hand, then he says, 'Don't hold that club too tight now.' Here he is, a thousand people around him, and he's focusing on me for that 30 to 60 seconds. It says a lot about the individual he is, the character he has."

Thirsk made the decision to retire from the club Feb. 1, 1993. He didn't quite make it that far.

"It was January 29, when a limo pulled up in front of our house," Thirsk said. "My wife, Audrey, and I got in, and there were pastries and coffee in there. The next thing I knew, we were off to the airport. She had my luggage ready, and we were off for two weeks in Maui.

"She didn't want me driving down that drive (to Kansas City Country Club) for the last time. She didn't want me to have to go through it."

T I P S

THE DRIVER

The driver is the most important club in the bag.

If you don't put yourself in position to put it in the fairway, you face an uphill battle all day long.

People get too careless about ball position. When hitting a driver, it is imperative to be forward in your stance. Because the ball is teed up, and you are sweeping at it, you are attempting a minimum amount of backspin.

Also, never use the driver first when warming up. As

Thirsk shows the position of the ball for a drive...

...and long irons and short irons.

golfers grow older, the risk increases of tearing a muscle if you warm up first with the driver. It's like having dessert first and then getting around to the main course later on.

So stay away from it on the driving range until you have tried the other clubs in your bag.

CLUBBING

If you truly are serious about golf, it is imperative to have your clubs fitted.

If you don't, it's like a carpenter without a hammer, nails and saw. Fit your needs because everybody is not the same.

The Average Joe should build his bag with a 4-iron through the wedges. A 5-wood, 7-wood and driver with 12 degrees of loft should be included, as well as the putter.

I am not a fan of the 1-, 2- and 3-irons. You're talking about a club with very little loft. You've got to know what you're doing. You've got to bring it fast and hard and you're not going to do it with a 1-iron.

The 5- and 7-woods are more important to your repertoire than a 3-iron. The woods are easier to swing.

Former *Saturday Night Live* star Chevy Chase (*Caddyshack* character Ty Webb) broke all the rules of golf etiquette, according to Thirsk.

"That's not the clubs I know."

THE COUNTRY CLUB
LIFE—THE FICTION

The 1980 movie *Caddyshack* is a big slice of Americana.
But is it accurate? Were the scenes genuine, possible,
impossible, true-to-life? Stan Thirsk, who knows a few
things about life in a country club setting, did his best Gene
Shalit imitation to offer his thoughts on the flick.

Read on.

First of all, Thirsk had to address the mechanical gopher
that Carl Spackler (actor Bill Murray) chased but never could
catch at Bushwood, the name of the fictitious club.

"I never saw one. I saw traps set at various courses, but
for moles," Thirsk said. "They had prongs on them. They
were trying to guillotine them."

The scene in which Murray's role had him popping the
tops off of tulips as he fantasized about being at Augusta
National Golf Club ("it's in the hole!" Murray proclaimed),
had Thirsk laughing hysterically.

Thirsk took exception to one of the opening scenes,
where actor Michael O'Keefe's character, caddie Danny

Noonan, was working for actor Chevy Chase's character, Ty Webb, and they were conversing about Noonan's future. Thirsk said that type of banter is extremely rare, and really isn't part of the caddie's place.

"I didn't talk that much (when I was a caddie). I was told to be quiet unless I was asked a question," he said.

Chase later wore a blindfold, with O'Keefe watching, and he told his caddie, "Feel nothing, hear nothing." Thirsk laughed, and began to shake his head again.

"If you don't have feel, you're not going to be able to play golf," he said, "at least not very well."

Another scene that bothered Thirsk was the caddie who had the cigarette hanging off his lips. He insisted that would never be tolerated at a club. Actor Ted Knight, who played the role of Judge Smails as the overbearing and snobby member, was worse than any member Thirsk ever encountered.

"I've seen people like that, but on a lower scale," Thirsk said. "I never had to deal with anybody that obnoxious."

Judge Smails, as the movie details, had a penchant for cheating. How often did he kick

Actor Ted Knight played snooty Judge Smails.

the ball away from a tree to give himself an improved lie? Lots.

Thirsk said those types of incidents are rare. "I once saw a guy who was up against a tree, and he took his club, with the toe out, and flipped the ball away from it (the tree) so he could swing. I mentioned it to the people he was playing with. But they already knew about it."

One of Thirsk's favorite characters was Rodney Dangerfield (Al Czervik), because of his outrageous behavior.

One of the most outrageous scenes in the movie occurred when comic Rodney Dangerfield's character, Al Czervik, owned a golf bag that was equipped with a built-in radio. He turned it up loud on the golf course.

How often do you see that?

"I've never seen that," Thirsk said. "It wouldn't happen, wouldn't be allowed. That's crazy."

As for the scene in which Chase was urinating just off the putting green, Thirsk cackled. "I've seen that done before, but at least the people who did it had the courtesy to go behind a tree," he said.

In the same scene, Chase was barefoot. That never would happen, Thirsk said.

"There are all kinds of chemicals on the greens," he said.

Bill "It's in the Hole" Murray (Carl Spackler) destroyed Bushwood Country Club in his efforts to catch the gopher, a mission that went unfulfilled.

"You don't go out of the locker room without your shoes."

There was a scene where O'Keefe was trying to putt, but was being intentionally distracted by noise and talkers. Thirsk said that isn't unusual.

"I've seen people cough, or bang their clubs against each other, at inappropriate times trying to distract the person they were playing with," he said.

One of the funniest scenes in the movie, although it is taboo, was the man playing in the storm with Bill Murray as his caddie. The man, thrilled when he sank an improbable putt that had some unbelievable backspin, lifted his putter skyward in exultation. At that moment, a lightning bolt dropped from the sky and struck the club, leaving the man for dead. Murray slinked off, as if he knew nothing about it.

Thirsk laughed, although he knows in real life that would not be a humorous incident. "We would never allow anyone to play in lightning. I've seen people who would have continued if we would have let them. You might not get a 'mulligan' if you try to play in that stuff."

Then there's Chase, who was tuning up his game by

playing at night. Thirsk said he can't recall anyone playing that late, but he wouldn't be shocked if it had been attempted.

"If they did, I don't think anybody would know about it," he said. "We did play nine holes once with these special lighted golf balls. It was neat."

The gambling that occurred near the end of the movie, in which $20,000, then $40,000 and ultimately $80,000 was wagered, well, Thirsk never heard of that much being bet at any club he was employed.

"It (betting) goes on, but nothing like that," he said. "You'll see $1 and $2 'nassaus' a lot."

During the final scenes, Chase knocked a ball into a tree that a bird snagged in its beak and carried away. Ever seen that? "No way," Thirsk said, "but I have seen birds get hit by golf balls and killed."

In the climax, Noonan's putt rested on the lip before Murray tried to exterminate the gopher by setting off the explosion. Thirsk said it never should have counted. At least it wouldn't these days.

"That thing was there for more than 10 seconds before it dropped. I don't think they had a time limit back when they made the movie," Thirsk said.

In conclusion, Thirsk liked the movie for its laughs, but didn't see it accurately portraying a place like Mission Hills or Kansas City Country Club.

"A lot of slapstick," he said, "but that's not the club or clubs I know. It was farfetched. You're not going to blow up your golf course. And the guy Ted Knight played....the membership would calm him down. The club is for all its members."

TIPS

THE PUTTER
("IT'S IN THE HOLE!")

The most important aspect of putting is controlling the distance.

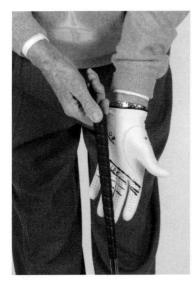

For putting, the club shaft fits in the palm.

Distance is more important than line. I can be two feet off line, but if I've got the distance right, I should be okay.

What controls distance? Shoulders and arms.

When you set up over the ball, you want the club up in the palm. That keeps wrist movement to a minimum. (This is different from a regular grip, where the club

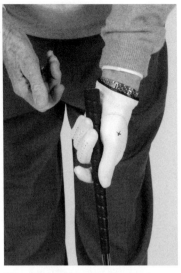

This changes the grip, allowing less flex in the wrists.

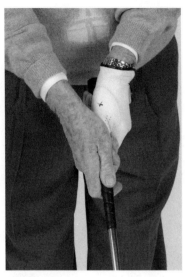

The right hand forms a "V" that aims up the chin.

Your stance should be parallel to your line, with the ball inside your lead foot.

You should be able to look straight down at the ball.

rests at the base of the fingers.)

As for your eyes, I like them to be right over the line to the hole.

The stroke should be like a pendulum, using your arms and shoulders. The back stroke and forward stroke should be the same.

Always get a close look at the green before you putt on it, checking for undulation. That observation is a key.

Of course, it is taboo to be above the hole when you putt. You want to be putting uphill.

THE ARGUMENT

Two legends from different sports—baseball's Ted Williams and golf's Sam Snead—once had an argument that I like to keep in my memory bank. I see it as a testimonial on how precise and unforgiving golf can be.

Williams and Snead went fishing in Florida, and they got into a big argument about which game is more difficult. Williams told Snead he only had a fraction of a second to determine what his eyes saw when the ball was coming to the plate.

But Snead said, "You don't have to play your foul balls when you hit them, and I do."

"Duke told me I could be in the top-10"

ULTIMATE TEACHER — NOT A BAD PLAYER

Stan Thirsk is best recognized for his teaching skills. He was honored for it in 1980 when the PGA of America named him its club professional of the year. The award was initiated in 1955. Thirsk is still the only club pro from the Kansas City area to receive the award.

He was anything but cocky about the honor.

"I always felt if a guy is the pro at a club, and is doing his job well, then that's what he's supposed to do," Thirsk said.

In 1995, *Golf* magazine named Thirsk one of America's top 100 teachers.

The lessons learned, in golf and in life, made his work worthwhile, Thirsk said.

"Golf teaches you all the right things in life. You play golf by the rules. You play life by the rules," he said.

Thirsk will tell you Duke Gibson was probably the best club pro in Kansas City. Gibson worked at the old Blue Hills

Thirsk had enough ability that he could have made a good living on the PGA Tour if he had chosen that career path.

Country Club. Thirsk hung on every word that came out of Gibson's mouth. That may have helped Thirsk become a factor when it was time to play with the big boys.

Thirsk was no slouch on the golf course.

"Duke told me if I played full time (on the PGA Tour), I could be in the top-10," Thirsk said.

Thirsk has played in 19 majors, including the PGA 10 times and the U.S. Open nine times, between 1958 and 1980. When he made the Open cut in 1963, Thirsk became fodder for one of the most famous columnists in sports history. Jim Murray from *The Los Angeles Times* wrote a piece about how Jack Nicklaus missed the cut in the Open. Murray wrote:

"Now, I take it, the main purpose of the cut is to lop off

COURSE RATED 72.	DISTANCES ARE FROM PERMANENT TEE MARK TO GREEN CENTER								
HOLE	1	2	3	4	5	6	7	8	9
DISTANCE	394	117	415	227	425	173	498	538	340
PAR	4	3	4	3	4	3	5	5	4
HANDICAP	7	17	1	13	5	15	11	3	9
STAN THiRSK	3	3	4	3	4	2	4	5	3
HERMAN SchARlu									
DUKE Gibson									
SANdY SchARlu									
John ThoRPE									
LADIES PAR	4	3	5	3	5	3	5	5	4
HANDICAP	9	17	5	13	7	15	1	3	11

PLEASE REPLACE DIVOTS — REPAIR BAL

the no-chance characters cluttering up the fairways. In this case, they eliminated Nicklaus to keep the course clear for the likes of Stan Thirsk, Ross Coon, Jr., Davis Love Jr., Ted Makalena and Bill Ogden."

Love, by the way, is the father of Davis Love III, 1997 PGA Championship winner at Winged Foot.

Thirsk later would appear in Murray's column again. In 1966, Murray wrote how "all the giants of golf were there," and, in tongue-in-cheek fashion, tossed Thirsk's name in the mix.

At times, however, Thirsk's game had to be taken seriously on a major stage.

He was tied after two rounds in the 1965 Bob Hope

9 - 3 - 63

OUT	10	11	12	13	14	15	16	17	18	IN	TOTAL		
3092	414	405	209	396	215	382	416	540	366	3343	6435		
35	4	4	3	4	3	4	4	5	4	35	70		
	12	2	16	4	10	14	6	8	18		GROSS	HDCP.	NET
31	3	3	3	4	3	4	4	4	3	31			62
34										31			65
37										36			73
40										39			79
37										39			76
37	5	4	3	5	3	4	4	5	4	37	74		
	14	8	18	2	16	6	10	4	12				

MARKS ON GREEN — RAKE OUT TRAPS

Some of Thirsk's best friends witnessed his course-record 62 at Kansas City Country Club in 1963. His best round at KCCC was a 61, but it was from the silver tees.

THAT'S T-H-I-R-S-K—

Thirsk Takes PGA Lead, Although Last Off Course

The New York Times   SPORTS

Allin, Thirsk Lead

DAILY NEWS, Indio, California   Friday, August 4, 1972

Palmer Only One Shot Back As Unknowns Grab Early PGA Lead

A lead at the end of the first round of the 1972 PGA Championship earned Thirsk headlines across the country.

Classic. He eventually dropped to a tie for seventh. Thirsk finished ahead of a few familiar names, such as Gene Littler, Miller Barber and Charles Coody.

Thirsk's reward for a job well done? Nothing much compared to today's big bucks. He made $2,850. Tom Watson's dad, Raymond, took a photo of Thirsk and that check.

In 1972, Thirsk created a stir in the first round of the PGA Championship at Oakland Hills Country Club in Birmingham, Mich. His 2-under-par 68 placed Thirsk in a tie with Buddy Allin after 18 holes. Most reporters had filed their stories when Thirsk was finishing near sundown. He birdied the 17th and parred the 18th. It was a rarity that day that anyone reached the finishing green in two.

But Thirsk got it done. He called his 3-iron to the green his best shot in a major.

"I can remember that (shot) and the drive. I killed them both," Thirsk said. "I hit the second shot against the wind, too, and it was overcast and misty."

Thirsk recalled later that night how his emotions rumbled through his body.

"I tried to have dinner, but it didn't go down very well," he said. "I must've turned over 1,000 times in bed."

Before his second round, Thirsk dined on orange juice, crispy bacon, dry toast and milk. The milk probably soured when Thirsk promptly 3-putted for a double bogey on the first hole. He posted another double bogey at No. 7. On the 16th, Thirsk built a snowman (an 8). By that time, it was obvious he was melting.

Thirsk shot 82, and barely made the cut.

"I did it all myself," he said. "I didn't control that thrashing inside of me very well at all."

Thirsk, though, said emotions and butterflies and nerves should be how you feel when you play. The key is how you handle the situation, and he admitted in the case of that PGA Championship he failed to handle it.

"If you're not keyed up, you're not going to do anything," Thirsk said.

A devoted family man, Thirsk chose his family and Kansas City Country Club over life on the Tour. Trying to be a

Thirsk earned less than $3,000 for his seventh-place finish at the Bob Hope Desert Classic in 1965. He only wishes he had earned a check comparable to a seventh-place finish by today's standards.

club pro and tour the country is a trick not even Thirsk wanted to attempt. He knew touring pros always would have an edge over him in that scenario.

"While (the pros) were hitting balls, I was teaching people how to hit balls," he said.

Although Gibson tried to convince Thirsk that he could've been a talent on the Tour, rubbing elbows with the big names in the game, Thirsk really wanted no part of it.

"There were things more important than whether I made the cut at the Podunk Open," Thirsk said.

All it took to prove that to him was a phone call one night, when he was on the road playing in a tournament.

"I called home, and my little girls said, 'Daddy, when are you coming home?' That put a big lump in my throat," Thirsk said. "I think I could have made a good living on the tour. But you have to pay in a lot of different ways that I did not want to pay."

Thirsk's daughters, Gay and Jodie, remember a father who was gone a lot. But when he came home, they were his focus. He let them know it by his actions.

Even their friends knew it.

"Dad was known as the Gum Man," Jodie said. "He would come home with a pocket full of Wrigley's Spearmint gum, and he'd hand out wrapped sticks to the kids. When he got home, the kids in the neighborhood would flock to our driveway."

Jodie recalled the times her dad would bring her to the club for lunch, and she would feast on chicken sandwiches and Shirley Temples. Later, she'd drive a cart, even if she wasn't supposed to be behind the wheel. Her father gave her clearance. Jodie never really developed a love of the game, however.

"I played junior golf until I was about 11," she said, "then I got interested in boys."

Jodie remembers her father as being kind and understanding.

"He's a good Christian man. He has the patience of Job," she says. "It takes a lot to get him riled. He's just loving, caring, wonderful. Even if I weren't his daughter, I'd say that about him."

Gay, the older daughter, didn't totally embrace her life as the daughter of a club pro. Stan would be busy at the club, and

Thirsk may no longer be able to compete on the professional tours, but he still shoots his age with regularity.

particularly in the summer, it caused her to miss some opportunities her friends experienced.

"I would see other kids go on their summer vacations," she said, "and I'd be kind of envious. He truly loved what he was doing. I was happy for him but kind of sad for myself."

Stan would make up for the lost time whenever he could, Gay said. She cherished Mondays, because he was off that day.

"He'd take us to Villa Capri. We'd get treasures out of the treasure box they had for the kids," she said. "Other times we might go to Smaks and get a hamburger. Monday was family day."

Although Thirsk wasn't always there, Gay never completely felt shunned.

"He's a great dad. He was always encouraging, uplifting," she said.

Audrey Thirsk knows as much as anyone the solitude that accompanies the life of the club pro's family.

"It was hard to accept, being left at home, with the children," she said. "Stan would be gone six days a week and on holidays and weekends."

Audrey felt that part of the problem was that Stan was so giving and caring that people at times would take advantage.

"Stan doesn't know how to say no. He can't say no to anyone, anytime," she said. "Somebody would want a lesson, and he just couldn't say no, no matter the time of day."

Still, she's enjoyed her life with Stan, and says she'd take the same path again if given the choice.

"Would I do it again? Yes," Audrey said about that life, which included trips to Augusta National Golf Club, the British Open and other trips that came courtesy of Thirsk's ties to Tom Watson and the generosity of Kansas City Country Club, which sent the Thirsks overseas to see Watson. "I'm pretty fortunate to be married to somebody as good as he is."

So Thirsk chose to pick his spots to show his golfing skills. When he continued to play in the most difficult settings, he showed he could handle it. He won the PGA Senior Club Professional championship when he was 52. A member of the Kansas Golf Hall of Fame, Thirsk still teaches at golf guru Jim Flick's schools.

The man could play.

From the time he eagled the 408-yard par-4 eighth in the first round of the 1971 PGA Championship to the 62 he shot to set a course record at Kansas City Country Club (Watson broke the record with a 60 in 1990), Thirsk never lost a desire to be the best player he could be.

And he never took the game, or its values, for granted. In 1990, Thirsk disqualified himself when he realized he had signed an incorrect scorecard after he had won the Kansas Club Pro Championship. It was the right—and only—thing to do, Thirsk said.

Perhaps his biggest thrill was one of his holes-in-one at No. 2 at Kansas City Country Club. The witness? Watson.

"I can still remember Tom saying, 'It's in!' I just stood there with my mouth open," Thirsk said. "I said, 'That's better than putting.' Tom smiled. As far as he was concerned, that's what we were shooting for. It's supposed to go in."

It's still going in. Thirsk, who shot a 67 the year he turned 70, always is striving for a low round.

"This old dog is always trying to get better," he said.

TIPS

THE FAIRWAY WOODS

If there is a club that may prevent you from losing all hope off the tee, it's the 3-wood. Especially when you're just learning the game, it's a good club because it gives you a little more loft. If you miss-hit it, it won't create as much sidespin as the driver. If you keep it under control, it will give you confidence. As your skills get better, go to the driver.

For females having a difficult time off the tee, I suggest a 5-wood.

THE LONG IRONS

Your set-up will go a little further forward of center. Your weight will go toward your right foot and leg. Here's some advice: Trade in your 2- or 3-iron for a 5-, 6- or 7-wood. They're easier to hit. Most people don't have enough speed to hit those irons. Use them for alignment. Don't let your ego get in the way and try to hit them.

TEACHING THE GAME

As an instructor, I take my role seriously.

When people are putting their trust in you, it's a big obligation. They all wish to get better. If we stay with the fundamentals, they should get better. It might be painful at times, but it will get better.

Change doesn't come overnight. Doing the correct things on the golf course can take years.

You learn, and the things you learn grow on you. Just because you put your hands on the club the right way doesn't mean you're going to have the right feel every time. It's something you just keep doing over and over and it comes to you in time."

There's a thrill people get when they do it right. They can't wait to get out there the next day. But it can knock you flat, too. You don't have that same feel every day. That's when you've got to keep a cool head and realize some days it will feel like you've got a pair of boxing gloves for hands.

This game is funny. I've had bad warm-ups, but when I got out there under the pressure, the feel would come. Other days I felt good and got out there and couldn't do a thing once I got on the course. Welcome to the game of golf.

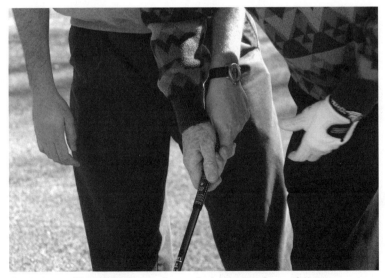

Thirsk devoted himself to his teaching, which kept him from a full-time career on the Tour. But he loves taking someone with little talent and improving his or her game.

"He seemed to know what to do."

His Prized Pupil

A smile immediately lights up Stan Thirsk's face when you mention Tom Watson. The feeling is mutual.

Both men throw the word love out there a lot when they speak about each other. They share a bond that has lasted through the years, during the ups and downs, the major championships, and victory droughts.

Through it all, they've stuck together. Thirsk and Watson. Best friends. But it's more than that.

"I love the man like a father," Watson says.

Thirsk wasn't sure, but he thinks the first time he laid eyes on Watson was in 1957. Watson's grandmother was a member at Mission Hills Country Club when Thirsk was working there. The club held a pitch-and-putt contest, and Thirsk remembers Watson's involvement in it like it was yesterday.

"Here was this little guy, 7 or 8 years old, and I saw how good his balance and rhythm were," Thirsk said. "Perfect."

Thirsk's relationship with Watson—a father-and-son-type bond—has allowed them to experience some of golf's greatest treasures like Pebble Beach.

A young Tom Watson kept his focus on Thirsk, who recognized the youngter's talent and determination at an early age.

That separated Watson from others in his age group.

"Usually, kids are going to swing with everything they have," he said. "Tom didn't. He seemed to know what to do, everything from his set-up to his swing. Needless to say, he won everything that day at the contest."

Before Thirsk entered Watson's world, Watson's father, Raymond, was the driving force behind his son's game. Thirsk said Raymond was a 1- or zero-handicap.

"It rubbed off on Tommy," Thirsk said.

When Thirsk took the head club professional job at Kansas City Country Club in 1961, it didn't take long for him to become a factor in Tom's world.

"He was as nice a man as there could be," Watson said. "I loved the game. He knew I loved the game."

Thirsk recalled how a young Watson had that look which made him easy to love.

"Mr. (Bob) Willits and Tom's dad called him Flytrap Finnegan (a 1930s cartoon strip character dubbed the world's worst caddie). He was this little kid with red hair and a jillion freckles. He was always talking," Thirsk said with a laugh. "He had this little space between his front teeth. Cute little kid."

The older gentlemen soon invited Tom to play along: Thirsk, Willits, Bob Busler, Jack DeWeese and Raymond Watson.

On his own, on days when the men might be at work, young Tom arrived at the club by 8 a.m. Thirsk said Watson spent hours daily at Kansas City Country Club in his youth,

Thirsk never had a son, but he says Watson filled the role admirably.

playing holes until he knew them like the back of his hand. Thirsk, who helped teach Watson the basics, recalls seeing Tom do the things necessary to evolve into a champion.

"The kids weren't supposed to play on Saturday afternoons, but we gave him a special exemption to play with us," Thirsk laughed. "He'd watch us close. Willits was a good wedge player. Raymie (Tom's dad) had a good swing. When I set up, he'd see I had a straight line with my left arm all the way down. Tom said, 'My dad told me to get my set-up just like yours.'"

Watson cherishes those days, and still talks about them often.

"It was a great treat to be with them," he said. "I was honored to be invited."

Thirsk said Watson yearned to learn, and that hunger eventually made him a champion.

"He'd be hitting balls off to the right because his grip was too strong. Then, he'd start hooking it," Thirsk said. "He would learn. It might take a while. One thing I admired about Tom was that he was smart enough to sort out stuff, and not just try to do anything."

Watson said Thirsk showed him how he used his legs too much with his swing, and that he got the club face in the shut position at the top too often. Watson began to figure it out, adjust, and improve because of it.

It didn't take prodding, promises or anything else to

ensure Watson knew what it took to be one of the best.

"I'd watch him," Thirsk said, "and after he'd finish a hole, he'd pull four or five balls out of his pocket and throw them in different areas and chip and putt."

There was a goal for each ball, Thirsk said.

"He'd say to himself, 'I've got to chip this in to win the Masters.' Or, maybe it was to win the PGA. He wasn't just hitting balls," Thirsk said. "He did this day in, day out."

Thirsk would see Watson intentionally hitting balls into the trees, so he could practice knocking them under or over limbs, using his imagination to overcome any obstacle.

Watson also was eyeing Thirsk. He knew a good thing—make that swing—when he saw it.

Watson, teacher earn PGA honors

Stan Thirsk gave a red-haired boy named Tom Watson golf lessons when he was 11 years old. Thirsk has watched Watson develop from a youngster with potential to the greatest player in professional golf today.

Thursday was a banner day for both.

Watson, for the fourth straight year, was named the Professional Golfers' Association Player of the Year. Thirsk, who completes his 20th year as pro at the Kansas City Country Club this season, was named the PGA Professional of the Year.

"It means a lot to me watching him develop and accomplish all the great things he has," said Thirsk, one of the top pros in the area.

And indeed, it was a great year for Watson. He won seven of the 23 tournaments he entered, finished in the top 10 in another nine and won a record $530,808. That bettered his standard of a year ago when he won $462,636. He had triumphs in the British Open, the

Tournament of Champions, Byron Nelson Classic, World Series of Golf, San Diego, Los Angeles and New Orleans Opens.

Watson has credited much of his success to his practice in the off season. Most of that work comes under Thirsk's watchful eye at the KCCC.

"I find the only way to improve is dedication to practice," said Watson after he won the World Series in August. "I practice a lot in the off-season. I only get away from the game in November. If you get away from it too far, you find it's a long way back."

Though Thirsk was not at all surprised at Watson's honor, he did not expect to hear about his own award.

"Yes, I was surprised," said Thirsk. "I didn't expect it at all. Mr. Cardi (Frank Cardi, president of the PGA) called me with the news this afternoon. I don't know if I deserve it, but I'm very happy. It's a nice little thing for me."

Stan Thirsk   Tom Watson

1980

1980 was a banner year for Thirsk and Watson.

Thirsk says Watson had so much natural ability that Stan's mother could have taught him to play, and she didn't play golf.

"Stan had a beautiful golf swing. I believe Stan has one of the most beautiful golf swings there ever was," Watson says. "I didn't emulate his swing as much as I admired it."

For all of his wins, major championships and honors, Watson never matched Thirsk in one particular category: hitting greens at Kansas City Country Club.

"I've seen Stan hit all 18 greens (in regulation). I have never hit all 18 greens in my life there. Ever," Watson said. "He'd go out and shoot 64 or 65 all the time."

Watson would listen to Thirsk. Most of the time, at least, Thirsk said.

"More than anything, when he was younger, we worked on his grip," Thirsk said. "If I tried to show him something, and he was stubborn about it, he'd want you to show him, prove to him, that it was a better way of doing it. There's nothing wrong with that."

Watson wishes he had paid more attention to Thirsk years ago.

"I probably could have been a better player if I listened more, and incorporated things he was trying to tell me. I was stubborn," Watson said.

One of the things Watson learned to do well at a young age was the bunker shot. Thirsk said he learned by watching Jay Hebert hit out of bunkers, and he included that in his teaching. Watson was his best pupil, and quickly picked up on it.

"We laid the (club) face open, stood the club right up

early, cocked the wrist early," Thirsk said, "then pop it (ball) up so it came out nice and soft."

All of the lessons that Watson learned from Thirsk came in handy one day in 1965 at Brookridge Golf & Country Club in Overland Park. Watson, just a teenager at the time, participated in an exhibition with Thirsk and Brookridge club professional Bill Knapp. The fourth member of the event was Arnold Palmer.

Yep, that Arnold Palmer.

"Tom hit the ball first, and he just killed it, right down the middle of the fairway," Thirsk said. "Most kids under those circumstances would be shaking in their shoes. Tom just looked at the gallery. He loved it."

By the conclusion of the event, Palmer walked up to Thirsk and made a prediction that would come true.

"He told me, 'We're going to be hearing from this kid,'" Thirsk said.

Palmer was so impressed and so taken with Watson that he sent him a set of golf clubs.

Watson had a way of using golf clubs unlike anybody else his age in Kansas City. When he participated in golf games at Kansas City Country Club, Watson came out on top more often than not.

"They'd tease Tom, said they were going to beat him like a drum," Thirsk said. "He'd just smile."

Thirsk and Watson often played "call shot." One player

Watson impressed Arnold Palmer (background) at an early age, and the legend remained a fan.

would call a shot, and the others had to match it. That type of game helped Watson down the road when he would find himself in a duel with the Jack Nicklauses of the world.

"He'd hit a low, cut slice or maybe a soft hook," Thirsk said. "You better know how to play that shot. If he can play it and you can't, he's got the advantage. Tom learned to play a lot of shots."

One of the games of "call shot" stands out in particular in Thirsk's memory.

"Tom and I were playing, and it started to rain on the 14th green, so when we went to 15, everybody hit a tee ball and we were off," Thirsk said. "The last guy in had to buy lunch.

"Tom and I were going along neck and neck until we got to the 17th. He hit a big, high-swinging hook into the crab trees. I hit mine in the fairway. I got a little ways out down the fairway, and I started waving back at him. He was still looking for his ball when I went to the 18th green."

Needless to say, Thirsk beat Watson into the clubhouse. Watson, though, got in the parting shot.

"When he got in, he asked, 'Which number cart does Stan have?' When he heard I had No. 1 and he had No. 2, Tom said, 'Next time, I want No. 1 because it's faster."

Another game they played was to take a 5-, 6- or 7-iron and try to hit shots the same distance. "You've got to do that by feel," Thirsk said.

Watson long has been known as a good rotten-weather

player. Thirsk said he got that moniker by playing in less than ideal conditions at Kansas City Country Club.

"He got tendinitis by beating 2- and 3-irons on the frozen ground. But he didn't back off," Thirsk said. "He practiced like Tiger Woods and Vijay Singh do now. He wanted to be the best. He knew there were no shortcuts."

Preparing to play by enduring elements that ranged from blustery winds to sleet, Watson used it to his advantage when he was entered in the British Open. Watson won five of them. It proved to be a combination of skill and survival that put Watson over the top so often on the other side of the Atlantic Ocean.

His preparation back home, starting so many years ago, allowed Watson to take advantage of the circumstances and his opponents.

"We'd play on days when the ground would be frozen," Thirsk said. "We'd play bump-and-run, sail everything in from the moon."

In the end, that strategy paid off for Watson in the British Open.

"He said, 'You know, Stan, I found out watching these guys, when the weather turns bad, some of them give up,'" Thirsk said. "Tom said the weather over there may have been bad, but compared to some of the rounds he played in Kansas City, it was a lot better. So his mindset wasn't affected at all by the weather. When we played at home, we never considered the weather. If the course was open, we played."

Thirsk is like a second father to Watson, who lost his dad in January 2000 after Tom had joined the Champions Tour. Thirsk has been there for the good times and the bad and often accompanied Watson to events.

After Watson won his first Masters in 1977, he called Thirsk later that evening. Watson's words were a glimpse into what he thought of Thirsk.

"He said, 'We really did it, didn't we?' I said, 'Yes, you did,'" Thirsk said.

Of course, Watson could have been referring to Bruce Edwards, his long-time caddy who died April 8, 2004. Thirsk and Edwards often were there together at majors, standing nearby as Watson spent time on the practice range.

"When Tom was warming up, he'd (Edwards) look at me and say, 'Did you like that?' I'd shake my head yes or no."

Edwards, who learned in 2003 he was suffering from ALS, was the epitome of a caddie, Thirsk said. "To me, he was never down. He'd get upset sometimes the way (Watson's) putter reacted. But I never saw him down. He always had the perfect yardage. From any point, he knew how far it was to the pin. Tom admired him. I admired him. People may not know this, but Bruce was a pretty good player. He had an exceptional eye."

Thirsk knew how much Watson thought of Edwards. It was a similar relationship to the one that Thirsk and Watson formed so many years ago. "When Tom would win, he would say, 'We won the tournament.' It was the two of them, in his mind," Thirsk said.

One event that Thirsk regrets not attending was Watson's stunning U.S. Open championship in 1982 at Pebble Beach, when Watson chipped in at the 17th for one of the greatest moments in golf history.

"I jumped straight out of my big chair in the family room," Thirsk beamed. "I'd seen him chip in a lot, so I probably shouldn't have been surprised. He's always done everything with a purpose."

Thirsk was touched and honored in Oct. 1992, when Watson spoke about him during Thirsk's induction into the Kansas Golf Hall of Fame.

Watson never forgot what Thirsk meant to him. A perfect example was in 1993, when Watson was captain for the U.S. Ryder Cup team. He named Thirsk his assistant. The day Watson called to ask Thirsk to join him stands out.

"I was in a state of shock. I finally got my voice and said, 'I'd love to,'" Thirsk said.

Watson saw Thirsk's addition as a no-brainer.

"He loves the game with a passion. People who love golf love to be around Stan because he loves the game so much," Watson said.

The event that year was at The Belfry in England, and Thirsk's room was right across the hallway from golfer Fred

Couples. Thirsk recalls that guards were posted at both ends of the floor.

No doubt the Ryder Cup has evolved into one of the most anticipated golf spectacles. Thirsk saw how important it was in his week in England.

"Every night, we'd all have dinner together and talk about the next day," he said. "People got tense. Players had been playing strictly for themselves, and now they were doing it for their country."

Watson, Thirsk remembered, passed European Ryder Cupper Nick Faldo and his caddie Fanny Sunesson, and said hello. Watson still is waiting for the response.

"Tom said, 'Good morning. How is everybody?' There was dead silence," Thirsk said. "This is your life. This is the Ryder Cup. Tom said to them, 'So this is how it's going to be?'"

The U.S. went on to victory. Thanks to Watson, Thirsk was part of it.

"I wasn't playing, and I wanted to win in the worst way," he said. "I got a beautiful cashmere sweater, beige, with the trophy on the front of it. I don't wear it very often. Only on special occasions."

Watson and Thirsk have had something special going for years. They still play and practice together. Before Watson headed to Hawaii to open the 2004 season, he met up with Thirsk for a round and practice. The learning never, ever stops with these two.

"We stayed on what we always stayed on—the fundamentals," Thirsk said. "Grip, posture, rhythm. Tom got pretty fast for a while, but we've tried to tone him down."

Watson's honesty is something Thirsk respects.

"He's a straight shooter. He doesn't throw you any curves," Thirsk said. "There's nothing phony about him."

No wonder Thirsk doesn't mind being a surrogate dad to Watson. In fact, he cherishes the thought. On a recent occasion, Watson whisked up Thirsk, and they were off for lunch at Steak n Shake. Some things in life may change. But not this relationship. It has remained strong through the years, a bond that never weakened. In fact, it only grew stronger.

"He's like my own son. I never had a son," Thirsk said. "I love him."

Watson feels the same way. That should be pretty obvious by now.

"Clearly, I was in awe of the way Stan played, the way he conducted himself," Watson said. "He was a gentleman to everyone he met. He never offended anybody. He treated people in an honest way. I still love going out with him to play."

T I P S

The Wedge

Concerning the wedge, ball position must be back toward the center or just a fraction behind it, and to the right.

When you warm up, it is crucial to use wedges first in the routine. I call them little-bitty swings.

In the course of a round, you're going to have to get up and in a lot, and you better have a good wedge game. When you practice with them, they give you a feel for the game.

The stance for a wedge shot has the feet close together with the ball position back in the stance.

The backswing is short.

THE SHORT GAME

Grip is a big deal with bunker shots and flop shots. A key to both is to weaken the grip a little bit.

When you're getting closer to the green, you don't want to be too "handsy," because moving your hands too much may cause you to decelerate on the downswing and all the way through the swing.

Spend as much time as possible on the short game because it is where you save strokes.

When you get close, you've got to be very precise. You don't have a 40-yard fairway to work with. It takes practice to be good around the greens.

The swing is almost all arm, with very little wrist movement.

Glide the hips forward at impact.

If you are playing a par-70, use the following approach. It should make clear how important the short game can be to your score.

You've got 34 field shots and 36 putts, so putting is more than half of your shots. So, you better have a very good short game if you don't hit every fairway and every green.

In terms of chipping, you should be back in your stance, with your hands and arms forward. That allows you to have the descending downswing you are looking for.

Also, don't follow through more than needed. That becomes a problem when a golfer uses too much wrist and hand action, trying to loft the ball in the air, and the follow through goes too far. Think of it as a quick bump and run, using anything between a 5- and an 8-iron.

In pitching, it should be the opposite effect. While chipping is less air time and more roll, pitching is more air time and less roll.

Your weight should be more evenly distributed in the pitching part of the game. There also should be more wrist involvement than there would be in chipping. It calls for a very light grip, just soft hands on the club.

The ball comes ever so slightly forward in your stance.

A 60-degree wedge, sand iron and pitching wedge is suitable for this aspect of the game.

BUNKER SHOTS

Tom Watson is one of the all-time greats when it comes to bunker shots. He learned how to do it the hard way.

Back in the 1950s, I'd get in a bunker and I'd ask (Blue Hills club pro) Duke Gibson, "How do I get out of this?" He would say, "Keep getting in, and you'll learn how to get out."

In time, thanks to keeping a close eye on Claude Harmon's style, I discovered a weak grip proved to be the correct starting point. Then, put the ball forward in your stance. Your hands? Put them behind the club head. Your weight should be on the left side. On the backswing, cock

Start with a weak grip and the ball forward in your stance.

Cock the wrists immediately. Turn the hips as you come back down

the wrists immediately. The face of the club should be pointing at your back (at the top of the backswing). Come back down, and turn the hips. That leads the hands all the way down.

"If he keeps (it) up he could be the best."

THE IMPACT OF TIGER WOODS

There's no doubt about it, according to Thirsk. Tiger Woods roared, and the entire golfing universe stopped to look and listen.

The Tiger Effect has taken on a life of its own.

Thirsk was among those watching closely. Except for a few instances during Woods' early years on the Tour, Thirsk indicated all the private investigators in the world would have a difficult time detecting anything wrong with Woods' game.

"When I first saw him, I didn't like all the fist-pumping," Thirsk said about Woods' penchant for showing emotion after sinking a putt. It became Wood's hallmark in the major championships during his breakthrough years.

Thirsk credits Woods' dad, Earl, for molding a champion.

"His father would do things to distract him, disrupt his concentration. He toughened up that kid," Thirsk said.

Thirsk did not like the "fist pump" when Tiger Woods broke onto the scene, but he found little else wrong with his game.

How many times have we seen Woods, in swing mode, stop at the top because of a camera click? Thirsk is amazed at Woods' ability to stop in mid-swing when that happens.

"I never have seen anybody, when you've got thousands of eyes on you, be able to stop on the way down," he said. "That's how much control he has."

Woods reminds Thirsk of somebody extremely close to his heart.

"He's like Watson used to be. His work ethic is why he's so good," Thirsk said. "You can tell the ones who want it bad enough, and Tiger's got it in him. I think he loves to beat balls. The good ones usually do."

Once Woods learned to control his distance with the irons, Thirsk said the phenom rounded out his game. Young players can learn plenty by watching Woods, Thirsk says.

"They (TV commentators) talk about how fast he turns his hips out of the way. What people have to realize is his grip is perfect, his posture is perfect. Those are the things they don't stop and think about. His fundamentals are perfect. Perfect balance. Perfect posture. Perfect grip. Perfect alignment."

Woods has matured, Thirsk noted, and that also impresses him about the man who is being touted as the player expected to challenge Jack Nicklaus' record of 18 major championships.

"He conducts himself as a class guy," Thirsk said. "He makes no excuses. He's made so many people more aware of

Woods has such torque on his swing that he creates great distance and control.

golf. That's got to be the greatest thing he has done so far."

Will Woods go down as the greatest ever? Thirsk says it's possible. But only time will tell.

"He does things you can't teach. He knows how to win," Thirsk said. "He's been doing this since he was on TV (*The Mike Douglas Show*) when he was 2. Even back then, he had a beautiful swing. If he keeps this up, he could be the best. It will be fun watching him try to become that."

TIPS

HOW TO START THE SWING (ROUTINE)

Getting started right starts with the left hand. That's the master hand, the first hand on the club, and it does the guiding and the controlling. Grip it right. Visualize the shot. Stand behind the ball, visualizing the shot. Set the target line.

It's all about establishing and following through on a routine. The first thing I'm going to do is aim the face of

Proper balance and alignment allow for a smooth swing...

...which is critical since the whole swing takes less than two seconds.

the club. Set the club down. Plant my left foot. Waggle a time or two to take tension out of my hands and arms. Move your feet in place to give you a little rhythm. It also helps keep tension from building.

You'll notice the pros always approach the shots the same way. They have a routine that puts them into a position to make their next shot.

THE SWING

The swing should be done without much thinking involved.

The whole swing, start to finish, takes less than two seconds. You'd better have your swing in order because you don't have time to change anything.

I've seen more people swing too fast than too slow.

Bob Murphy stops at the top. I wouldn't recommend his rhythm. He's won, but I don't see anyone else pausing at the top. You don't stop and then go. The swing is continuous. Using a continuous swing will give you consistent speed, which gives you consistent shots.

How to Hit it Far

Everybody wants to hit it as far as Tiger Woods. A wide arc helps distance. Hit it squarely on the face of the club with the maximum amount of club-head speed without exceeding the speed limit and without giving up balance. If you try to swing the club faster and harder than you can control, you're in trouble. It's just like going 80 on the highway—you have a chance of getting a speeding ticket.

This speeding ticket will cause you to wind up in the woods, in the sand or water, or just plain off-course.

"These guys want majors."

THE BEST
OF THE BEST

Asked to rank the 10 greatest players of all time, Thirsk offered this:

1. Jack Nicklaus
2. Sam Snead
3. Ben Hogan
4. Tiger Woods
5. Bobby Jones
6. Byron Nelson
7. Arnold Palmer
8. Gary Player
9. Tom Watson
10. Billy Casper

The Dream Fivesome. Some of the all-time best golfers played at Watson's Children's Mercy Classic (clockwise from left: Gary Player, Arnold Palmer, Lee Trevino, Jack Nicklaus and Tom Watson).

Thirsk based much of his top-10 on major championships.

"These guys want majors. If you don't believe it, just ask them," Thirsk said. "Having never won a major, I only can go by what I hear. You don't remember those guys for winning in Florida or Philadelphia. You remember them for winning the Masters and the British Open and the other majors.

"These rankings are based strictly on how they played. I considered the difficulty of the tournaments they were playing. It takes a little bit more when you're competing in an Open. The courses are set up to play more difficult.

"It's also based on how many tournaments they won, even if they weren't majors. In my opinion, if you're playing against the best in the world, that's major.

"Not only does this reflect their ability to play, but there's something inside that allows them to compete and stand up under pressure."

Thirsk didn't rank Tiger Woods higher because his career is incomplete. He wouldn't be stunned, though, if Woods makes it all the way to the top some day.

"If he continues to work at it, he'll be No. 1," Thirsk said.

Finally, with the exception of Bobby Jones, Thirsk saw each of these men play. He even had the opportunity to play with five of them (Snead, Palmer, Player, Watson and Casper).

JACK NICKLAUS

Until somebody else wins 18 major championships, Thirsk considers Jack Nicklaus the greatest player of all time.

"He dominated like nobody has to this point," Thirsk said.

Thirsk noted an equally impressive number for Nicklaus: 19. That's how many major runner-ups Nicklaus recorded. To be in the hunt so often, and to come that close to winning it, makes Nicklaus extra special in Thirsk's eyes.

"He didn't have as pretty a swing as (Sam) Snead's, but it was good enough," Thirsk said.

One of Nicklaus' second-place finishes proved to Thirsk just how good the Golden Bear was. The year was 1977 in Turnberry, Scotland, for the British Open. Nicklaus and Watson went head-to-head in what is considered by many as the greatest down-the-stretch golf duel in history. Each man was making remarkable shots, bombing in putts from enormous distances, and doing it all day long in the final round.

Watson had the upper hand, needing a par on the 72nd hole to win. He looked safe for the winner's circle because Nicklaus nearly had driven his tee ball out of bounds. His second shot, from rough that could hide a puppy, was spectacular. Nicklaus miraculously reached the green, and for good measure, drained a long putt to put the pressure on Watson, who practically had a gimme to finish off Nicklaus. He did so, concluding a day of dramatics that won't soon be forgotten, if ever.

"Nicklaus showed us what he was made of that day, even if he didn't win," Thirsk said. "He had the stuff on the inside that isn't visible."

SAM SNEAD

Snead was one of a kind, Thirsk says.

Sam Snead

"As far as I'm concerned, he had the most beautiful swing I've ever seen," Thirsk said. "I haven't seen anything before or since like it. A lot of guys have come close. Julius Boros, Ernie Els, Retief Goosen. But ask all the older players, and they talk about Snead. He had the rhythm."

Snead's 81 PGA Tour wins, the most in history, says it all, Thirsk said. The only major he failed to win was the U.S. Open. Snead accepted some misinformation in the 1939 U.S. Open, and thinking he needed a birdie to win when all he needed was a par, went on to triple bogey the hole and lost.

"He didn't keep playing. That was his mistake, and it really cost him," Thirsk said.

BEN HOGAN

One thing that impressed Thirsk about Ben Hogan was the fact that he didn't try to do more than he was capable of doing.

"I remember one year when he won at Oakland Hills on a beautiful iron shot into the green and two putted for the win at the U.S. Open. Everybody talked about what a great shot it was. He said it wasn't all that great, but his concentration was. He knew he had to do it, but he knew he could do it, because he practiced it over and over.

"He never tried to play something that he hadn't practiced before. Using today's terminology, he 'stayed within himself.'"

That approach impressed Thirsk, even early in life.

"When I was a kid," Thirsk said, "I always chose the Boston Celtics, Joe Louis and Ben Hogan. He thumped everybody just like those others I mentioned did.

"I'd say to the other kids, "I get to be Hogan, or I'm not going to play.' He was my idol because he wasn't very big," Thirsk said. "I was 97 pounds in high school.

"I loved the way he concentrated. He and Nicklaus were the best at playing like they were out there by themselves, and nobody else was with them. He got to where he could do everything."

TIGER WOODS

Woods could become the greatest of all time, Thirsk said, but he still has to complete the journey.

"There's no telling what he might do. He's a physical specimen," Thirsk said. "He's the new way they play golf. Flexible. Athletic. Strong. He has the modern swing."

The Woods phenomena even has affected Thirsk.

Tiger Woods

"We're all talking about him. I think he really has learned to handle it beautifully," Thirsk said.

Before he turned pro, Woods also won six consecutive amateur championships (three U.S. Junior Amateurs and three U.S. National Amateurs). Those titles have to be considered as part of his exceptional record.

BOBBY JONES

The reason Bobby Jones is listed this high is because he was the best player of his era. When he won his seven majors (as an amateur), he did it against the best amateurs and professionals as well. He could have been higher if he had decided to turn pro and continue his career for many more years, rather than retire as an amateur at age 28.

Bobby Jones

The greatest amateur champion of the pre-modern era isn't someone Thirsk got to see. But he heard so much about the man that Jones is impossible to ignore when considering the greatest in history.

"I know he had a beautiful, fluid swing. He was a smart man who didn't make many mistakes," Thirsk said. "He helped start the Masters. Thousands of people are enjoying what he in part got going at Augusta. He's a legend."

BYRON NELSON

"When you consider Byron Nelson's record and the fact that he retired a full 10 years before Ben Hogan did, you have to include him in this list," Thirsk said. "Just think of the tournaments that he could have won if he had kept playing."

Nelson's string of 11 consecutive victories in 1945 is a feat that probably never will be duplicated. It's a record that stands alongside Joe DiMaggio's 56-game hitting streak in baseball as special performances. "What Byron did was unheard of," Thirsk says. "His stroke average was just 68.33 for 120 rounds, an all-time record. You can't have many rounds over par and do that.

"It's hard to imagine anybody — even Tiger — would dominate like that again.

"He's another hero to me. He was more like the average Joe than most celebrities. He was called the king of the irons. Duke (Gibson) told me

Byron Nelson

Byron was such a good iron player because he drove the ball perfectly."

ARNOLD PALMER

"What can you say? He was the king," Thirsk said of one of the most popular golfers of his day. "He was like Elvis (Presley). They were comparable. One was the king of music; the other was the king of golf.

"I remember being paired with Arnold in the PGA in Dallas (in 1963), and there must have been 10,000 people around the first green. That was Arnie's Army."

Palmer was known for his great desire, and as a competitor, he didn't back off from anyone. "Whenever he could promote golf, he did," Thirsk said. "He did so much for the game, and he introduced a lot of people to it because he was so visible.

"He was so accommodating to the gallery when we were playing. I'll never forget that. He never, ever forgot the galleries. He loved them as much as they loved him. He did everything for golf.

"He also looked out for the people he was playing with, whether they were fellow greats or fringe players like me. He is just a great ambassador for golf."

GARY PLAYER

What sticks with Thirsk about Player wasn't solely his ability to be one of only five players to win all four majors.

It was Player's body.

"He worked out, worked so hard at it. He put more effort into building his body than anybody, and not a lot of guys did that back in his day," Thirsk said. "When you looked at the scores in the majors, he always seemed to be up near the top because he was such a good ball striker. He was little. But he was gritty."

TOM WATSON

Watson was Thirsk's star pupil.

"Tom had so much talent, my mother could have taught him — and she didn't play golf," Thirsk said.

What makes Watson among the best, Thirsk said, were the five British Opens that he won.

"The courses over there can be so difficult, then you add the weather into it, and it's so difficult to play at times," Thirsk said. "He was able to stand up to the pressure."

Watson's determination set him apart from the haves and the have-nots. "He didn't back off. He wanted to get better," Thirsk said.

Thirsk began giving Watson lessons in his pre-teen years, so he knows a little bit about what made Watson tick. Thirsk couldn't be more proud of what he became.

"It made me happy to see him do well," Thirsk said. "He did it all by himself."

Tom Watson

BILLY CASPER

"He didn't get the press he should have because he was overshadowed by Arnold Palmer, Jack Nicklaus and Gary Player," Thirsk said. "But he was right there with them."

The statistics back up that thought. Casper won 60 tournaments (51 on the PGA Tour and nine more on the Senior Tour, almost the same number as Palmer (70, 60 on the PGA Tour and 10 more on the Senior Tour). A couple of those were U.S. Opens (1959 and 1966) and another was the Masters (1970).

"He competed really well with them," Thirsk said. "He was just not as flamboyant as they were. He also battled a weight problem and allergies. He played under a pretty severe handicap, but he played beautifully.

"He could turn his ball left to right. He could putt. He knew he could putt."

TIPS

THE SAND WEDGE VS. THE PITCHING WEDGE

What's the difference in approach to a sand wedge as opposed to a pitching wedge? You get a lower trajectory with the pitching wedge. If I have 100 yards to go, and the pin is on the back, I'm going to use a pitching wedge because I can go at it with a lower trajectory. If the pin is on the front, I use the sand iron to get a higher trajectory so it (the ball) will stop quicker and won't roll as much."

The object of bunker shots is to get it out of the trap.

It takes a quick elevation of the club head...

...a full backswing...

...to pop up the ball...

... and get it to stop quickly.

SHAFT LENGTH

How do you choose the proper shaft length for your clubs? If your arms are shorter than normal, you might need extra length. If your arms are long, you might need shorter clubs. The club is an extension of your arms. The length of your arms needs to be considered with club length. But very few people need different clubs. Standard length will fit most people.

HITTING OUT OF THE WOODS

The best way to get out of the woods is not to get in them. But we all end up in there once in a while. Stop and check the possibility of getting it through toward the green. It might be best to take your medicine and chip out to the fairway. Don't try to exceed your ability in this situation. That may help keep you from making a lot of triple bogeys and quads. If you'll just be safe and get it out, who knows? You might knock the next one on the green.

BACKING UP AND APPROACH SHOT

If you swing down on the ball with enough speed, it will cause the ball to back up. Just follow the rules of pitching.

The clubhead should hit the ball slightly above the equator.

The ball is back in the stance to cause the club to descend quicker.

The hips drive forward to help elevate the ball.

"This close."

THE BEST OF THE REST

Any Top-10 is a subjective list. It's hard to argue with opinion. But even Stan Thirsk had some tough choices to make in preparing his top-10. Here are thumbnail sketches on those who rank among the all-time greats, just not in his top-10 (in alphabetical order).

JIM COLBERT: "I remember when he lived in Kansas City and was playing on the Tour. He had trouble getting his ball two feet in the air with a driver. But he always had such a good short game, and it really began to benefit him on the Senior Tour. Jim had the insides, the will to win, and it really showed once he hit 50."

Jim Colbert

Vijay Singh

Fred Couples

FRED COUPLES: "If he hadn't had back problems, who knows how much more he could have won. Even with the problems, he still could swing the club beautifully. He won the Masters, and that always is special. But it seems like he won most of his money in those made-for-TV Skins Games. He made millions doing it."

BEN CRENSHAW: "Everybody can try to emulate his beautiful putting stroke. The rhythm of it, and the pendulum-like stroke is perfect. When he won the Masters for the second time (in 1995, shortly after the death of his golf teacher Harvey Penick), it was so emotional."

Ben Crenshaw

JOHN DALY: "When he won the PGA (in 1991), he had a great, big, long swing. The thing that impressed me most about that was how he still was able to control it. He almost hit his left ankle on his backswing, but he brought it back down on line. He also has a soft touch with the wedge around the green. The only thing that has held him back is himself."

John Daly

DAVID DUVAL: "I think he's fallen so far because of his grip. He has his left hand way over to the right, and he's got to change that. He's got the talent. I have to believe he'll get straightened out, if he wants to. If he gets it going, it will be something to watch his comeback. He still could win a lot because he's young."

ERNIE ELS: "Fantastic swing. His rhythm really is beautiful. You never see him out of rhythm. He stays within himself. I like the way he shows his confidence, and he won't back down. I don't see any glaring weaknesses in his game. Maybe the only difference between him and Tiger is how bad he wants it. I think Tiger may want it more. Tiger's there to do one thing, and he's that way every time. When Ernie's like that, he's tough"

Ernie Els

NICK FALDO: "He really could hit some nice iron shots. He worked at it. His win at the Masters when

Greg Norman collapsed always will stand out when you think of Faldo. He might have been underrated. He played really well. He won six majors, so when he was going well, he really had it going well. He never wavered when he got behind."

JIM FURYK: "He's got that unorthodox swing, where he takes the club on the outside and drops it down on the inside. He's modified it a bit, and he's become very effective at it. He's won a major, so he had to be pretty effective. Dick Mayer had a swing kind of like that, and he won the (U.S.) Open. Miller Barber swung it like that and he was a winner."

SERGIO GARCIA: "He's still young. He's going to do a lot of good stuff before he's done. He's made an improvement on his swing when he's coming down. He's also begun to control his waggling. He's competitive. He challenged Tiger at the PGA (in 1999 at Medinah) when he was 19. That said a lot about him, and that's when we learned so much about what he could be some day."

RETIEF GOOSEN: "I like him because he's a swinger of the club. He has the type of swing you should try to emulate. He won the U.S. Open, and he has the opportunity to win more. His rhythm is so good, and he has everything under control."

WALTER HAGEN: His 11 major championships rank second to Nicklaus.

"I heard he really knew how to get under a guy's skin without being too abusive," Thirsk said

Thirsk recalled coming across Hagen in a U.S. Open at Winged Foot, long after Hagen's playing days had ended. He may not have been in the spotlight any more, but Hagen still attracted attention.

"It was Mr. Hagen this, Mr. Hagen that. People still loved to be around him. Why not? He was a great, great champion," Thirsk said.

CHARLES HOWELL III: For no bigger than he is, he thumps the ball a long way. He's got a swing that will last, and he's very competitive. He's somebody to watch on the Tour. It's amazing he's so thin, but there's a lot of power inside there."

HALE IRWIN: "His iron play was kind of like Byron Nelson's. Both of them were so solid. He won the U.S. Open three times, so he had to be a good ball striker. You can't win that event three times on just luck alone. His swing is the same over and over."

Tom Kite

TOM KITE: "He did a lot with not too much to start with. He worked hard to get where he is. The guy never won a whole lot, but he won money titles by being so consistent and staying close to the top of the pack."

JUSTIN LEONARD: "He's not very big, but he gets a lot out of what he has. He won the British Open, and he can win it again. He has that modern-day swing. He's got the right temperament."

DAVIS LOVE III: He's not so young anymore, but I still think he's got some good golf left in him. I like his swing very much. Sometimes he can make crucial mistakes with the putter. He should be able to win more than he does. It was special when he won the PGA (in 1997 at Winged Foot). There's no reason why he shouldn't win more majors."

Davis Love, III

Phil Mickelson

PHIL MICKELSON: "He's got so much talent. I just don't understand his problem. He's just got his mindset on doing things a certain way, and that might have prevented him from winning the majors. He's definitely got the talent to do it. He has all the shots. He's had to endure as much criticism as anybody. He doesn't get it, but he will. It's taken a lot longer than it should have."

COLIN MONTGOMERIE: "He let the spectators, particularly at the U.S. Open, get to him. They'd give him plenty of flak, and he could give it right back. That's his problem. If you're really into your game, you block that stuff out. He couldn't always do it. He's trying to figure out who made a comment, when he should be thinking, 'Who cares?' He couldn't handle it."

Greg Norman

GREG NORMAN: "For a while there, he was the best player around. He was at the forefront of the game. He had the ability, but he was snakebitten. He got disappointed so many times. He's had some really tough luck. Faldo beat him in the Masters after Greg built a big lead on the final day. Larry Mize got him at the Masters, too, with a shot out of this world. Bob Tway knocked in a shot out of the bunker (in the PGA Championship) to beat him. Greg learned it takes 72 holes."

NICK PRICE: "He's got good control of his clubs. Good swinger. He's had some trouble with putting, but not much else was wrong with his game. In the 1990s he was as good as there was. He could go head-to-head with anybody."

ADAM SCOTT: "Watch him. His swing is almost exactly like Tiger's. He does everything very, very similar to Tiger. I really like his swing. He's good, and I think Tiger will have his hands full down the road because of him."

GENE SARAZEN: The man won all four majors, one of five to do so. "He was a husky man, kind of built like Watson, but huskier," Thirsk said. "His double eagle at the Masters was unbelievable. It's a shot everyone knows about."

When Sarazen played the Masters long beyond his best years, it was obvious to Thirsk that Sarazen had the goods.

"Even when he was older, you could see he knew how to put the club on the ball right where he needed it," Thirsk said.

VIJAY SINGH: "He never has been afraid to put in the work to achieve what he has done. I remember being up in Columbus, Ohio, doing a golf school, and Vijay was there. He'd be the last one to leave the practice area. It's why he swings so well and is so consistent. He was relentless."

Vijay Sngh

Curtis Strange

CURTIS STRANGE: "Curtis, for a couple of years, was fantastic. You just don't win two U.S. Opens in a row like he did. He had a beautiful swing that he kept under control. He also had a fire in him that I liked to see."

LEE TREVINO: "When it came to talent and playing shots, he could play more shots than anybody I had ever seen. He just had that charisma. People love him a lot. He was talking all of the time. I thought he was a very good broadcaster, and he was usually right. He was

Lee Trevino

funny and came up with things right off the top of his head. He won all the majors except the Masters. He had the game to play anywhere. Only Hogan, Nelson and Snead had a better array of shots than he did."

MICHELLE WIE: "She looks really good. She looks like the modern player, using the big muscles. She seems to have the composure. It's obvious she has the ability. I've seen her drain some putts we'd all like to make. I don't know if physically she could play with the men day in and day out. It would be tough for her to compete. But we should watch her."

Michelle Wie

MICKEY WRIGHT: "She was the best woman player I ever saw. I was fortunate enough to play in an exhibition with her at Blue Hills. Later on, I remember Ben Hogan said she had the best swing he had ever seen. Well, that was good enough for me. She could win, and she was consistent."

FUZZY ZOELLER: "I think he didn't mean to hurt anybody when he said those things (about Woods and the champions dinner at the Masters). He just always has his mouth going. Maybe that's why he whistles more now. The guy could play, though."

TIPS

SWING STRENGTH

When is it better to use a shorter club with a stronger swing, as opposed to using more club and less swing?

The alignment for a fade shot.   The alignment for a draw shot.

Because of uneven grass, morning dew and other potential obstacles...

...Thirsk says it's better to chip or pitch from a few feet off the green instead of putting...

Anytime you feel you have to force the club you are using to get it there, put it back in the bag and go one more. Make your normal swing. If you feel like you have to catch it really good to get it there, go one more club. Try to stay normal is the bottom line.

THE DRAW AND THE FADE

How do you hit a draw? Where does the draw start? To the right. Adjust your alignment to accommodate the shot. Take your grip, but before you do that, aim the clubface to where you want the ball to end up.

...The chip has a low trajectory and a lot of roll...

...while the pitch (pictured) has a higher trajectory and less roll....

How do you hit a fade? Aim left. But your club face would aim to the right. Just follow through with your normal swing.

Both are designed to get you close to the pin.

THE RIGHT DECISION UP CLOSE

When you're within a couple of feet from the edge of the green, is it better to putt or chip? Some days, your touch is really good. So you could do either. The thing may be what time of day it is. In the morning you may have a lot of dew, and it may not be smart to try and putt through it. You may want to take your 7-, 8- or 9-iron and chip over it. Just look at your circumstances.

"We're lucky to have him."

THE PRO'S PRO

What follows is an array of comments from people whose lives have been touched by Stan Thirsk. One thread, a common theme that runs through nearly all of them, is how wonderful the man is.

"I knew him years ago. I know he was very helpful to Tom Watson. If he helped Tom become what he is, he had to be good. Stan's a very nice person, very knowledgeable. It was very enjoyable to be around Stan."

Byron Nelson, legendary golfer

"He always would say, 'Feel that? Feel it?' He always had a twinkle in his eye when you were out there with him. I had a lot of people give me lessons, but they didn't have the eyes Stan has. He probably has the fastest eyes. He had a quick answer for what he was seeing."

John Hoover, who took lessons from Thirsk
at Blue Hills Country Club

"I don't know one person who didn't like him. He was the same when he came to the club as when he left. A real gentleman. The perfect guy, really."

Bebo Sloan, member of Kansas City Country Club

"I broke 80 this past fall. When I first started taking lessons from Stan, I was shooting in the high 90s and low 100s. He got me to change my swing. I used to take it back weird. We got that fixed. He got my right hand in the right place, too. From when I started two years ago, I know twice (as much) now."

Keaton Knott, a budding 14-year-old golfer

Donald Hall, Sr.

"He calls me the ninth wonder of the world because I have the most awful swing. I have a bad back, so when I swing it back, I go all the way around. If I had ball bearings on my feet, I'd do a 360. I didn't get into golf until I was married. I'd heard Stan was an excellent teacher. I'd play with him every now and then. His caliber of play was a little bit better than the others in the group. He used to call me Cash McCall because McCall's magazine gave me balls with McCall on them. I was playing with those balls the pro shop, so he gave me that name. But he is a wonderful gentleman. He had to be to play with us duffers. We were lucky at Kansas City Country Club because of Stan. Stan's kind of an institution."

Donald Hall, Sr., chairman of the board, Hallmark

"He won the national club pro of the year, and he's also won the senior club pro championship. To master both ... I don't know if it's ever been done. I have a lot of friends who have taken a lot of lessons from him. We're lucky to have him."

Rob Wilkin, club professional, Heritage Park Golf Course

"I called him Stan the Man. He didn't insist on playing with just the top golfers. He played with me. He created a greater democracy at the club. He's the only pro I know of who's welcomed at all times even if he isn't in charge any more. He was very generous offering his help to everybody. He helped Tom Watson. If Stan wasn't good, Tommy wouldn't have kept coming back asking for his help."

Graham Porter, Kansas City Country Club member since 1957

"I never took a lesson from him until this past year, but I found out he's the consummate golf pro. Most guys who are teaching golf don't know what they're doing or how to communicate. He (Thirsk) confirmed and reaffirmed what I wanted to do. He's just not complicated. We were out there one real hot day last summer—blazing hot—and he was locked in on me. If you book time with Stan Thirsk, he's locked in on you whether you're a hacker or Tom Watson."

Robin Cunningham, Kansas City businessman

John Sherman

"It was 1982, and it was something like 30 degrees outside. I was hitting balls at Kansas City Country Club. All of a sudden, Stan and Tom came riding up in a cart, and Stan said, 'John, let's see you hit it.' Stan was solid as a rock to me, and his support was a wonderful thing. You can't say enough good things about Stan. He was incredibly patient. Stan was the kind of guy who would work with you and work with you and work with you until you figured it out. He didn't just spend 45 minutes or an hour with you. He'd follow it up. If you had a lesson with Stan, you got your money's worth.

"You knew the man could play the game, and you knew the man could teach the game. I owe my success to Stan. I'll never forget, as a little kid, playing in the Pro-Junior with him at Liberty Hills. People were hitting 6- or 7-irons on this one hole, then he took a 5-iron and it took one hop into the hole for an eagle. It was the club for the shot as opposed to how far you can hit it. Play your game and play the golf course. That's how he did it. It made an impression on me.

"Oh, by the way, he eagled the next hole, too. When I made the cut in 1983 in the U.S. Open at Oakmont, the first person I called was Stan."

John Sherman, Trans-Mississippi champion in 1982; Kansas Amateur champ in 1981 and 1983; Missouri Amateur champ in 1984

"He loved to play with the ladies. He was wonderful. He would only tell you something if you asked him. He's probably one of the most genuine people I know. He just couldn't be a better person. When I come up with a good shot, I'll say, 'I learned that from Stan.' He's the best."

Jean Honan, 2003 club champion at Kansas City Country Club

"Every year around Christmas, Stan and his family and our family (wife Joan, daughter Susan, sons Chuck and David) had dinner under the old dome at the Bristol. The man is the consummate gentleman. When my wife got her first hole-in-one, Stan got her a plaque. How about that? He was thrilled. That's just how Stan was."

Chuck Battey, KC businessman and KCCC member

"I've known Stan for 40 years. Probably nobody loves the game more than Stan does. If you're hitting balls on the range, and you're having trouble, he just can't help but come help you. Tom Watson is a good testament to what Stan means. I wish everybody would be like Stan. I wish I was more like him."

Jerry Krause, Thirsk pupil

"I had never been a golfer until I was 61. I had worked all my life, and had never touched a golf club. My husband, Max, said he made an appointment with Stan for me to take a lesson. I said, 'Max, he won't teach me. I'm a nothing.'

"I couldn't even sleep the night before my first lesson. On the first day, he was such a gentleman. I'd actually taken a lesson in California, but it hadn't sunk in. Stan, though, taught me how to enjoy the game and learn the game. I'm not bragging on myself, but I was a 46 handicap, and now I'm in the 20s, and I've only taken lessons two years from him. I was playing in Arizona, and people would say, 'I don't know where you learned to play golf, but your form is excellent.' Even a retired golf pro there said it. I was so proud. I immediately thought of Stan. He's such a solid man, a gentle man with a beautiful soul."

Pat Foust, Thirsk pupil

T I P S

Choosing teh Right Shaft

What are the advantages to titanium, graphic and other shaft compounds? If the club is lighter, like the graphite shaft, you can get a longer shaft which gives you a wider arc. That helps generate more speed and distance. The graphite shaft is a big deal. It's why players are hitting it further and straighter.

Long Irons Off the Tee

When is it good to hit an iron off the tee (besides par 3s)? If you can drive the hole, hit the driver. But know your limitations. If you have water to the left and out of bounds to the right, you may want to use your irons. It's all based on the circumstances that you are facing at the time.

Whenever you have a chance to tee it up, Thirsk says you should. A short par-3 means teeing up a 7- or 8-iron, but that prevents anything from getting in the way of a correct hit.

TEE IT UP WNENEVER POSSIBLE

Should you use a tee for irons on par 3s? Any time you can put the ball on the tee, that's a perfect lie. You can't get any better than that. Otherwise, if you get blades of grass between the face of the club and the golf ball, it can do funny things.